EXECUTIVE, VENTURE CAPITALIST, AND ACADEMIC ENDORSEMENTS

Executives

"Kurt explains the concept of moving from   sales to business development through our experiences at Boku and anecdotes from other startups. At this crucial point of inflection, Kurt helped us at Boku, and I'm sure that you'll benefit from reading this book, leading your startup to success."

—JON PRIDEAUX, CEO of Boku

"This book is for any startup CEO, CRO (Chief Revenue Officer), or VP of sales/business development. It outlines a methodology on how to work with the largest companies in the world effectively. Kurt tells much of what we learned from a decade at Boku and some anecdotes from other companies; read it, and you won't need to go through the ups and downs we did."

—MARK BRITTO, EVP of PayPal and Founder of Boku

"At Boku, we were always 'bigger' than our 100-person startup seemed. The key was business development, where we did deals with multinational companies like Apple, Facebook, Microsoft, MasterCard, Sony, and more. Kurt has captured the step-by-step methodology on how we did it and how you can apply it to your company."

—RON HIRSON, former CPO of DocuSign and Founder of Boku

"Kurt does a great job explaining how Boku worked with Microsoft, educating us about a unique technology to seal the deal. Business development is not about taking clients to dinners or cocktails; it's about understanding customers' pain points by listening closely and offering them the right solution even if your company does not have it all, sharing both the strengths and weaknesses."

—MOIN MOINUDDIN, former Microsoft Payments Executive
and VP of Engineering at Fieldwire

"Kurt and I worked together during the social games days. He was an inveterate networker, always creating relationships but strategic in his approach. And he was relentless in always adding value to our partnership. He exemplifies BD at its best."

—MURTAZA HUSSAIN, Co-founder, President of Streamlabs
(acquired by Logitech)

"Navigate to the Lighthouse provides business development advice on a global scale, highlighting hard-earned knowledge from multiple companies about how to think about global expansion, successfully execute new market entry from Asia to Europe, and forge lasting, profitable partnerships."

—THOMAS CLAYTON, Chief Revenue Officer of Bill.com
and Global Technology Executive

"Hands down, this is the best book on business development in the market. If you are an entrepreneur, Chief Revenue Officer, or VP of sales trying to Navigate to the Lighthouse to more sophisticated, needle-moving deals for your startup, this book is a must-read. Trust me. As one of his old bosses, I've seen him do it."

—ARVIND NARAIN, Technology Executive/Investor and CEO at APIDefender

"Kurt's one of the most respected BD execs in Silicon Valley. His exceptional hustle is a necessary, but not sufficient, character trait; more important is the strategic work he puts into his 'landing lighthouses.' Now, he's written a very practical, much-needed how-to that lays out the technique he's used to drive dozens of significant deals to close."

—MARK JACOBSTEIN, Serial Entrepreneur with four exits
and Chief Business Officer at Immunai

"Navigate to the Lighthouse is an authentic, practical look at the thoughtful strategy, hard work, and stamina that it takes to build transformational business partnerships at any scale—including fundraising. Based on two decades of experience building successful international relationships in tech, Kurt provides a tactical guide on how to develop an opportunity, build relationships that create value, and make a lasting impact."

—MARK BEGERT, CEO of FabuLingua and Technology Entrepreneur

"For building multinational partnerships, Kurt succinctly provides decades of lessons learned in an easy-to-understand methodology in Navigate to the Lighthouse. We've worked together on cross-border deals while at Boku and my companies. If you have a desire to see how the international business world works and learn the skills of doing significant partnerships, this book is for you."

—MARK GERBAN, Multinational Technology Executive based in Europe

Venture Capitalists

"To be a Startup Hero, you have to close sales deals that ignite your business and then propel it to success with larger strategic business development partnerships. Kurt outlines how to do this with his experiences, other anecdotes from Silicon Valley, and actionable takeaways. Now it's your turn."

—TIM DRAPER, Founder of Draper Associates, DFJ, and Draper University

"I worked with Kurt when I was co-founder/CEO of TrialPay, and he was always persistently working on deals. Now he puts his technique and methods into a very thoughtful book. It's definitely recommended reading for any entrepreneur or startup person who's focused on 'big-game hunting'/transformational deals."

—ALEX RAMPELL, General Partner, Andreessen Horowitz
(venture capital investors in Boku)

"I will be recommending this book to all founders in our portfolio. Kurt pairs helpful frameworks with anecdotes that bring the theoretical to life. It's also chock-full of concrete tactics and tips that are going to immediately make anyone more effective in hunting their next lighthouse deal. I suspect this will not only be a helpful initial read but will become a frequently referenced guide for many founders and execs."

—EVAN TANA, Serial Entrepreneur and Founding Partner of Script Capital

"I have worked closely with dozens of founders selling to enterprises. Finding and closing lighthouse customers is one of the hardest and most rewarding milestones for an early-stage startup—it can make or break you. In this book, Kurt lays out a step-by-step guide packed with practical advice, real-life examples, and strategies to leverage everyone on your team—from VCs to executives to engineers—to help you win your lighthouse deals. It's a must-read for founders and startup execs who interact with enterprise customers."

—SAQIB AWAN, Partner, Lightspeed Venture Partners

"Navigate to the Lighthouse is a great explanation of how to move from a good startup to an outstanding unicorn. The explosive growth phase is where many entrepreneurs fall back on 'just fundamental sales execution' as a plan. Mr. Davis explains from experience how to create and execute a mindset for the next order of magnitude growth."

—GREG BAKER, Managing Partner, Towerview Ventures, a venture capital fund, part of Alumni Ventures Group

Authors and Academics

"Landing deals is key to the success of any business. In this smart, from-the-trenches guide, Kurt Davis shows how it's done, providing real-world advice to transform your business pipeline."

—DORIE CLARK, author of *Reinventing You* and Executive Education Faculty, Duke University Fuqua School of Business

"Kurt and I worked together during his Boku days, which are well documented in this book. He uncovers his secrets and acumen that closed many of the deals with my company and many others in social games. My book, Explosive Growth, focuses on the marketing tactics for success, while his book will help you achieve explosive growth through business development deals."

—CLIFF LERNER, Serial Entrepreneur, author of *Explosive Growth*

"Startup founders often think they just need to build a great product and the world will beat a path to their door! That's not enough if you want a successful outcome or to be recognized as a unicorn! You need a go-to-market plan, and that includes sales and business development; these roles are as different as software and hardware engineers. Your BD pro is more entrepreneurial and creative; most importantly, they aren't looking for lighthouses to retire this month's quota. Kurt outlines what you need to do and how you need to do it. This is a must-read for any founder, early revenue executive, or salesperson who wants to build a career in biz dev."

—DAVE PARKER, author of *Trajectory: Startup—Ideation to Product/Market Fit*,
CEO of Trajectory Media

"Navigate to the Lighthouse is a must-read for all levels of sales and business development teams as it lays out a detailed roadmap to understanding and developing successful business relationships. Kurt does a beautiful job integrating years of practical experience with critical negotiation theory. This informative and insightful book is a catalyst for moving the needle. Now go land your lighthouse!"

—JESSICA NOTINI, Principal of Notini Mediation, Facilitation & Training Services

"Kurt has a wealth of experience in the profession of business development. He has great practical advice and insight from having done it for decades. And he has taken the time to craft that into a concise guide for those who want to learn the art themselves."

—DEAN TAKAHASHI, Lead Writer for GamesBeat at VentureBeat

NAVIGATE TO THE LIGHTHOUSE

NAVIGATE TO THE LIGHTHOUSE

A SILICON VALLEY GUIDE TO EXECUTING GLOBAL DEALS

KURT DAVIS

LIONCREST
PUBLISHING

COPYRIGHT © 2022 KURT DAVIS

All rights reserved.

NAVIGATE TO THE LIGHTHOUSE

A Silicon Valley Guide to Executing Global Deals

ISBN   978-1-5445-3033-8   *Paperback*

           978-1-5445-3034-5   *Ebook*

To Mom and Dad (RIP—hope you are together now), you always wanted to know what I was up to, what was keeping me so busy, and why I kept traveling the world. Thank you for letting me live the life I wanted to.

CONTENTS

ACKNOWLEDGMENTS

Thanks to Jonathan Philips who helped me get all of this on paper during the pandemic. Without his support, it would still be in my head. If you'd like help getting your thoughts on paper, he's your man. Email him at jonathanphillips1818@gmail.com.

Then, over to Jessica Cyphers, who did a first-class job making my ADHD, hodgepodge manuscript coherent. ☺ She cut, reorganized, and distilled it into a legible and succinct text for you, the fast-moving, startup business audience. If you need an editor, she's your woman. Jessica.cyphers@hotmail.com.

Props to Andrew Means at Transom Design, a creative and design agency, for help on the illustrations. Thanks also to Ann-Sophie De Steur (annsophiedesteur@outlook.com), who designed the front-page lighthouse and a few other illustrations.

Thank you to my alpha reader Alberto Moel (VP of Strategy and Partnerships at Veo Robotics). He was my first avatar who painstakingly slogged through several drafts, providing me insightful feedback: "Focus on your target reader and cut out the fluff."

Special thanks to Jon Prideaux, Nicholas Reidy, Josh Wein, Gregg Delman, Thomas Clayton, and Ron Hirson, who all provided an exceedingly large amount of knowledge for this book.

In addition, thanks to the following executives, professionals, and entrepreneurs for your contributions: Mark Britto, Joanne Liu, Adam Lee, James Higa, Mike Ghaffary, Emil Michael, Richard Purcell, Mark Jacobstein, Mark Gerban, Jessica Notini, Dorie Clark, Kevin Grant,

Max Lehmann, Jason Spero, Dave Maynard, Ryan Paugh, Ricky Paugh, Tyler Epp, Junichi Fujimoto, Matt Eggers, Riccardo Zacconi, James Patmore, Ranjan Reddy, Faissal HouHou, and Stephen Lee.

INTRODUCTION

A proud young venture capitalist, turned startup COO, once told me, "Sales is constantly chasing, hustling, and closing deals, while business development is just shrimp and cocktails. You sit around and chat, make friends, and have some martinis. Maybe you do a deal, maybe you don't—either way, it's okay." I chuckled on my way out, as I very gently closed the door—click.

If you think business development (BD) is just overpriced martinis and chitchat, you likely haven't gotten the results you've wanted. I've spent vast amounts of time doing both sales and BD. I lost more sanity doing one than the other—and let me tell you: it wasn't sales. Spending a significant amount of your life (several years) on one deal may indeed drive you to drink; I certainly did my fair share.

Lucky for you, I can help you keep your sanity intact. Over the years, entrepreneurs have asked me about how to hire a BD Captain and measure their progress on deals that take a long time to close. Venture capitalists have asked me how to set up a global footprint. Chief Revenue Officers have asked how I moved deals forward and structured them so that they wouldn't sink the ship once they landed. The VPs of Sales asked, "How do I level up my game?" In response, I've written numerous blog posts about BD, negotiation, international expansion, and more. Thanks to the pandemic lockdown, I decided to go one step further and write this book to connect the dots backward (thanks, Steve Jobs).

The dotted line connects large deals with Sony, Microsoft, and Apple—to name the notable ones—that I worked on over eight years while working at a company called Boku. At that time, I knew what was and wasn't working, but I didn't draw a set of lines to success. Even now, I won't claim my BD strategy is foolproof, but I *can* tell you what worked well and what didn't, and maybe I can help keep you out of the bars and from taste-testing every new flavored vodka martini—stirred with a touch of lychee for me, please.

This book is about strategic BD and sales in business-to-business (B2B) technology. It's the sought-after advice you're asking for.

The strategic development this book propounds will touch on how to execute drastic changes through sales, strategy, storytelling, international expansion, corporate development, PR/marketing, and all the way through to closing. All are a must for a qualified strategic plan into which any investor will buy. These are the components of strategy you need to consider before executing BD and will make or break your business when navigating through the chasm. So, then, what kind of business does it apply to?

If you're a business that sells software-as-a-service (SaaS) software with a recurring revenue component and you're trying to increase the zeros at the end of your customer revenues, then this book is a home run. Regardless of the widget, if you are in a hypercompetitive global business, then this is a triple. If you are in hardware or another type of sales, you may hit some singles or doubles. If you are in business-to-customer (B2C), you may want to bunt, though you may find some information worth more than the amount you spent on it. B2C consists of techniques like growth hacking, A/B testing, ad words, conversion funnel optimization, and so forth. On the other hand, in B2B, customers must be found, relationships developed, and deals signed. This book focuses on businesses that need to sell their products versus products that are naturally sold.

This book's content inevitably bumps shoulders with one of the great books on managing tech startups, *Crossing the Chasm*. In *Crossing the Chasm*, Geoffrey Moore explains the technology adoption life cycle[1] by placing product adopters into three different groups: the early adopters, the early majority, and the late majority/laggards. When Moore wrote *Crossing the Chasm* in 1991, he explained the reasons for the first chasm between early adopters and early majority and advised how tech startups could make the leap and become relevant players. Moore's market analysis still rings true: many tech startups get stuck in the market of the early adopters struggle to get that next-level client. However, many of the book's recommendations on the nitty-gritty of crossing the business chasm are different today.

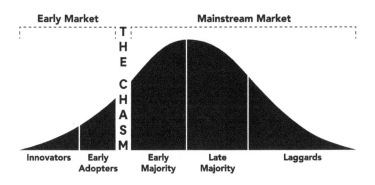

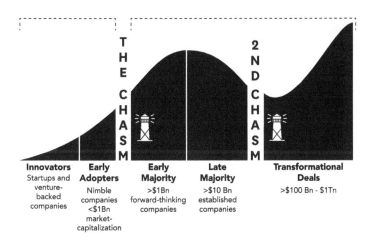

This illustration is taken from the book *Crossing the Chasm*.[2]

Simply put, the stakes are higher: companies raise money faster, go global at the speed of light, and build teams in the blink of an eye. With all of this going on, how do you cross the chasm without burning through all the money, churning through several different management teams, or being taken under by a strategic deal? If *Crossing the Chasm* is the what and why of bringing your startup to the next level of business, then this book provides the how—specifically, for catapulting across the chasms (yes, plural) in 2021.

In *Navigate to the Lighthouse*, not only do I discuss the first chasm, but I also cover the recently emerged second. Beyond the second chasm lies the land of the trillion-dollar companies—Microsoft, Google, Apple, and Facebook. If you manage to cross the second, you've reached the land of transformational deals. Many of the premises I discuss in this book apply to both chasms, but there will be a few critical differences when we talk about the second chasm—namely, crossing the first chasm needs a sales team of two or three. Closing a transformational deal and crossing the second chasm needs a whole company working in sync.

Either way, scoring the lighthouse deal is the first step.

What Is a Lighthouse Deal?

The objective of this book is to teach you how to leap the chasm by scoring an initial deal called the lighthouse, a common term in BD circles. Just as a lighthouse marks new land and opportunity, so does your lighthouse deal; it notifies all the players in a new market that you are a leader and qualified to play in that market. Once that deal closes, more will follow. Sometimes the lighthouse is the transformational deal in terms of revenue; more often, however, it is the stepping-stone that leads you to other transformational deals. Those deals will bring scalable revenue growth for your company and lead to greater sustainability. The lighthouse deal is the one that shines light on these new market opportunities.

The lighthouse deal takes time. Building your startup is a messy, grueling process that requires you to have short-, medium-, and long-term visions. Reading this book, you will learn how to position your company to level up and score more significant partnerships, thus increasing your business's potential. I once heard a venture capitalist say that there are only three types of startups: those that grow to a $10 million valuation, a $100 million valuation, and a $1 billion valuation. (Now there are even $100 billion—most recently, DoorDash, Stripe, and Airbnb.) Leveling up requires a company to make radical changes in how they approach deal-making. This book discusses ways to focus on both the medium- and long-term deals to bridge the first and second chasms.

Why Me?

I'm good at it. It's always better to be lucky than good, but I want to show you how to be damn good, if not the best. Luck is just a bonus, albeit often a very big one.

I learned how to hustle early in life. My success started with selling magazine subscriptions door to door in middle school and winning the sales championship three years in a row. The reward was a trip into the money machine—a makeshift box with a leaf blower that blew dollar bills in the air. Afterward, I leveraged my neighborhood connections and launched a landscaping business. That experience gave me a good foundation in the ups and downs of selling.

In 2000–2003, I started my professional career in finance in Hong Kong and learned the importance of analysis and sophisticated modeling. Later, I started a company in China selling mobile phone games to telecoms in Asia. Then, when I arrived in Silicon Valley in 2006, I married the skills of finance and sales to work on deals for startups. In 2008, I joined Boku Inc. and started hustling again.

The time at Boku provided me distinctive BD know-how. Boku was an unusual company in that the business was predicated almost entirely on BD deals. On one side, we worked with mobile phone carriers worldwide; on the other, we joined forces with digital media companies like Facebook, Google, Sony, and Microsoft. Our product was an API (application programming interface) that connected mobile telecom carriers' billing systems to third-party digital content companies' payments systems (like Apple) so that their customers could make payments. The product didn't sell itself, so we hit the ground running.

Let me reemphasize this point: the products didn't sell themselves; I had to sell them. This company wasn't a high-growth unicorn like Facebook or Uber that everyone was chomping at the bit to get a ride on; nor was it a Google or PayPal where salespeople can receive inbound calls and process multimillion orders. Instead, the businesses I worked for weren't even attractive or scalable at their start. I was one of the point people who made them viable. Starting from ground floor and building a startup that delivered a successful outcome gave me notable experience and an almost unique perspective on how to grow a sales and BD function from start to success.

Not only was Boku's business model unique, but so was my experience there, especially compared to other people in Silicon Valley. Highly unusual for a nonfounder, I rode out a startup for nearly eight years. I was Boku's first BD/sales hire, and we started small, closing deals that were only a few thousand—if even that—in revenues per month. Over the next few years, the Boku team exploded, closing hundreds of deals, including deals with telecommunications companies around the world like DoCoMo, KDDI, AT&T, Softbank, T-Mobile, Vodafone, and Telefonica; mobile games and applications companies like Electronic Arts, Rovio, Zynga, Supercell, and Kabam; and large technology companies like Sony, Microsoft, and Facebook. The capstone deal was Apple.

To accomplish this, I lived in Japan for three years (covering Asia) and in London for one year. I participated in, led, or worked with my team (whom you'll hear from in this book) to close many of these deals, generating seven and eight figures in revenue for a startup that was probably initially quite similar to yours. My tenure at the company, international experiences, and successfully closed deals across a spectrum of industries are all learnings that I'd like to share.

Boku's result was an IPO in London and $5 billion in transaction volume for a company that struggled through treacherous seas for many years. We were good; there was little luck involved.

You may question the relevance of this content since it dates from 2008 to 2016. History repeats itself: the setting, the product, and the industry may not, but the ways of people do. I've spoken to enough executives to know that what we did still applies, and I've updated the content as I have seen fit. For example, lead generation in a pandemic is quite different from networking at conferences, so I've added a section for that. At the end of the day (and many to come), the content remains useful.

If you'll excuse me for any apparent cockiness, I'm your man for BD on an international scale. Oh, and if you think I'm just chest thumping, I'm not. It's not all glory; I cop to my mistakes and explain them along the way. The missteps are how I've figured things out. But also, it's not *just* me. I've invited about 20 others to contribute, to augment my knowledge where I lack expertise and to provide fresh insight. In the spirit of team sales, this book is a team effort to provide you with a complete solution.

I've written this as a guide with three parts. Part 1 covers *the basics*, charting the course for your ship into stormy seas, and it consists of market analysis, strategy, and initial outreach. Part 2 is *the meat and potatoes*: it galvanizes the team for setting sail and shows you how to maneuver your ship. This part touches on the supporting functions you'll need from your entire team before going full steam ahead, including international expansion, corporate development, marketing and press, team sales, and planning. Part 3 is *the secret sauce*, explaining how to land the deal (ship) and expand. To do this, you need to know the five Cs of selling: consulting, collaboration, committing, closing, and customer success. These are the blood, sweat, and tears of BD. Master these, and you'll be well on your way.

Your time is valuable; in fact, nothing is more paramount than how a BD person spends time. I want you to employ these ideas and score big, so I'll keep it as pithy yet potent as possible. On my website KDAlive, you'll find links to example spreadsheets and deal plans. To make it easy to access these documents, I've inserted QR codes. Scan them with your phone camera, and they'll whisk you away to the referenced examples on my web page. Or when you go to KDAlive.com, click the "Entrepreneurship" tab on the menu at the top. You will find a box that says book links; go to that blog post, and you'll see the links.

As a side note, the idea for this book came to me while traveling through Africa. There, I taught at entrepreneurship hubs in Ghana, Nigeria, Kenya, Zambia, Zimbabwe, and all the daring way to a refugee camp in Kakuma, where we started a small venture capital firm called Kakuma Ventures (www.kakumaventures.com). While visiting these hubs, I saw a gap in the sales ability of many of these entrepreneurs, so I taught them what I knew about sales and BD. After writing an exhaustive presentation for those African entrepreneurs, I stitched it all together in this book. After all, to teach is to learn. Please read about my African adventure in my previous book, *Finding Soul: From Silicon Valley to Africa.*

Now grab a martini or your drink of choice, and enjoy.

PROLOGUE

It's funny how impending doom can refocus your business on what matters.

Nicholas Reidy (a contributor to the second half of this book), who was Boku's VP of Customer Success and my good friend, leaned back in his swivel chair, looked over his shoulder at me, and said, "You ran the tables—closed all the game deals, almost 40. There is nothing left. What do we do now?" I hadn't yet thought of what was next; we'd been too busy getting customers signed up and launched. Those deals, in addition to our deal with Facebook, wrapped up the online games market. We weren't worried just yet; we'd figure something out, I thought.

In my mind, the logical next step was to work on a different segment of the game industry, mobile games. After hosting a dinner party with 20 of these companies, we learned quickly that Apple and Google would take all payments in-house. How would we work with them? Where would we start? Whom do we even talk to? Those deals seemed impossible. I began to worry. Perhaps the entire business had no opportunity for growth.

There was a blinking light in the distance, however; Spotify showed interest in our payments, and Sony PlayStation was responsive to emails and meeting requests. Microsoft and Apple, too, responded to our inquiries but with no concrete steps forward. Our founder, Ron, was shuttling back and forth every week to see Microsoft in Redmond. Sometimes they'd meet him; other times he'd be stuck at a coffee shop waiting for a response. They were slow. How long could we continue like this before sinking?

The breeze shifted. Google moved into mobile carrier payments and created a new headwind with mobile phone carriers, which we followed. Apple had just announced a move into payments that gave us hope. Maybe, just maybe, we'd caught wind.

That was about the time that—as many companies do—Boku changed captains. The company went through an executive transition, bringing on a new CEO, Jon Prideaux. With his blessing, I went off to work on these lighthouse deals, and it was now my turn to shuttle around and wait in coffee shops. It became apparent that working with larger enterprises took a lot of time from the entire company, even our CTO and CEO. I needed their executive support to win.

These companies indicated that they wanted to partner, but their demands were excessive and took heaps of time. They wanted well-researched and supported data, specification documents, PowerPoints, proven technology with scale and reliability, and a partner who would serve them. Sometimes they answered our emails; other times they didn't. They sent us lengthy requests for proposals (RFPs) and were slow to respond to our answers. These discussions took years, and we were always doubting how to hook them. We had the capabilities, but sink or swim, we had to try. Heading toward those flashing lighthouses was the only option.

How does this story relate to your business?

Are you worried that you've tapped your initial market dry and need to scale to bigger deals or a new industry? Are you at a loss about how to approach bigger companies and what to say to whet their interest? Do you get anxious when they don't respond for weeks? I certainly did.

This position will force you into one of two actions: you'll either walk the plank and jump overboard, or you'll turn your doubts into adrenaline that will help you hold your course. You might feel panicked in these moments, but the way you channel that anxiety is what determines whether you will make it to the lighthouse or not. It's that extra energy that can help you break through to the next level. It's also the paranoia that may drive you to your wit's end; it all depends on how you react to it. And trust me, the paranoid don't survive.

What you'll read in this book is how I learned to channel my company's uncertainty and navigate to our lighthouse accounts. Through the crucible of closing seemingly impossible deals, we forged a sustainable business. My main hope is that the direction and structure I provide will spur your innovation and speed your startup's journey to enduring success.

PART 1

CHART YOUR COURSE TO THE LIGHTHOUSE

"Nail the Basics"

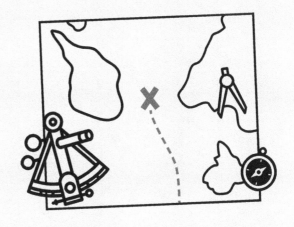

CHAPTER 1

SALES IS NOT BUSINESS DEVELOPMENT

"All salesmen are actors: their priority is persuasion, not sincerity . . . There is a wide range of sales ability: there are many gradations between novices, experts, and masters. There are even sales grandmasters."

–PETER THIEL, *Zero to One: Notes on Startups,*
or How to Build the Future[3]

Peter Thiel got it right when segmenting types of salespeople, but dismissing sincerity is plain wrong. There is no way to develop a long-term business relationship without sincerity and trust.

In this chapter, I'll focus on the part he got right: the three types of salespeople. Later, I'll discuss sincerity and trust. Novice salespeople create consistently growing and predictable revenue streams. To do this, the sales or go-to-market (GTM) team must utilize well-defined marketing, legal, and finance templates to close several deals a quarter against a pipeline. Sales should drive consistent growth in the organization through many small and medium-sized deals. These deals are done in the near term and provides instant gratification to the salesperson.

Expert BD, on the other hand, handles longer sales cycles and involves the executives, investors, and leaders from a company's many functions. Simply, the BD Captain focuses on the important at the expense of the urgent. With the goal to discover new market opportunities in new industries or geographies, they must find suitable product angles that will open doors and win deals in these markets. Success is closing a lighthouse in an untapped market, which signals to others that you are open for business. Once this is accomplished, you can open the gates to the sales team who can capitalize on similar customers while the BD team searches for the next lighthouse.

Going one step further, the masters, or those I will call captains, are those who spend an entire year or two closing one large lighthouse or transformational deal. They are the ones who think the impossible is possible.

In Chapters 1 and 2, I discuss restructuring your GMT team—sales, BD, and marketing—making it more suitable for pursuing large transactions.

To get started, you'll need to nail the basics. Detach your company's sales and BD functions, hire a BD Captain, and clearly define their differences. Let one or two people focus on the long deal cycles while the sales team continues to knock down smaller deals. Even this minor change could earn you millions or billions.

Know the Signs You Are Approaching the Chasm

Here are the key ones:

1. Your sales team isn't getting positive feedback from potential customers or is running out of prospects.

2. Increased pressure to customize deals. In sales, you should always use a standardized contract. Good salespeople sell what they have in a standard, shrink-wrapped product—no additional requests from product management needed. The reason for this is that it takes time to customize products and add new features. When your salespeople feel it's time to make product changes and customize, there's a good chance you are approaching a chasm or lighthouse account.

3. You're getting asked more detailed questions about your product capability, uptime, and future services. Presentations are getting more extensive, requests for proposals (RFPs) are longer, and meetings are involving multiple functions of the organization.

4. Your sales team is requesting support from different functions of the organization because they aren't armed with enough information to support the opportunities you're approaching.

5. The CEO, perhaps you, is getting pulled into more sales meetings. You may be wondering, "Why do they need me? Why can't they manage themselves?" The answer: to execute a lighthouse or transformational deal, you need to build relationships across an entire company. Increased demands of your CEO and your internal organization are both clear signals that the chasm is both near and bridgeable.

Who Are BD Captains?

Unlike hiring a VP of Sales, you don't hire a BD Captain to hit a quota. You hire a BD Captain to land lighthouses. While a good sales team maintains the constant growth rate of the company, BD ignites the growth curve by creating new lines of business.

WHAT ARE THE TRAITS OF A BD CAPTAIN?

Your ideal hire should be able to execute a long-term deal and fit into your culture. But how do you know if he can do both? Business hires can be expensive, so it is important to know what to look for.

You may ask about *personality type*. Although extroverts may stereotypically make better BD people, this isn't always the case. Introverts can also make good ones, as they tend to be thorough, conscientious, and easy to get along with. Instead of focusing on personality, I'd say find the person who fits your internal culture with the abilities and values below:

1. *They must have worked in a small company environment* without the support and bureaucracy of a large company. Venture capitalists dispute this point. Some say it's best to hire someone who has fought it out at a startup; others will only hire

someone who already has an extensive Rolodex and has done many deals. The thing is, it's much simpler for someone at a billion-dollar company to get deals done—everyone wants to deal with them. But just because someone has worked for a big company doesn't mean they'll come through with a deal. A good BD leader continuously looks for ways to change and grow. They come up with ideas, analyze prospects, and make swift decisions. These skills aren't often learned at established companies but at other startups.

2. *They have a track record of closing.* They can play both the short and long games for market-beating outcomes. They may hit doubles or triples early in the business game, but after that, they only hit home runs and grand slams. Many BD people scroll through a Rolodex of big brands with little to show for it. Others chase small deals to pad their résumé or to show the executives they are getting deals done. Either way, both can be a distraction to your startup. The best BD Captains know how to say no and only work on deals that matter.

3. *They understand the product.* This hire may not have an engineering or product background, but they must understand enough of the complexities to speak intelligently about it. This is important because you don't want your product or technical sales team to have to sit in on every meeting. I used to read over technical documentation and sit with product managers for hours to understand our capabilities before meetings.

4. *Slow chess is their game.* Judge a business developer by how he or she thinks and interprets the market. Having some understanding of economics, game theory thinking, and market dynamics are Business Development 101. These people are on the front lines talking to customers, networking at conferences, and following the industry. Steering product direction is essential for victory. They don't have to beat the latest AI computer, but they must be thoughtful, even perspicacious.

5. *They are effective communicators.* Although knowing the intricacies of sales is critical, your ideal BD person must communicate

with a variety of people in many different situations. They'll need to wear many hats: a trust builder, a collaborator, and a closer. They'll work with people in procurement, legal affairs, marketing, and sales, and with executives and on boards. They need to be flexible and patient. They should be able to develop trust by knowing how to act and what to say. In essence, they need to know how to woo the client.

6. *They understand legalities—a bonus.* Some of the most successful BD people in Silicon Valley, like Emil Michael (Uber) and Mike Ghaffary (Yelp) who contributed to this book, have legal backgrounds. The ability to wordsmith contracts that work to your advantage can save your company millions. (Barring this, you must have a patient lawyer—thanks, Javier.)

7. *They've spent time abroad or traveled significantly.* Without this, it will be challenging to relate to people in Silicon Valley, let alone in other parts the world. With the explosive growth of companies globally, this person will likely be traveling a lot. Ideally, they have both lived abroad and worked domestically.

8. *They are clairvoyant.* They see, hear, and identify market openings where others don't. In Y-Combinator's startup questionnaire to founders, they ask, "What do you understand about your business that other companies in it just don't get?" If this were a BD question, it would read, "What market opportunity have you identified that others have not?"

9. *They are transparent.* Nothing is worse than a BD Captain who oversells the executive team. If a deal is falling through the cracks, they need to be honest and escalate the risk to the CEO. Obscuring the status of a lighthouse deal deserves a demotion right out the door.

WHEN YOU SHOULD HIRE

Most nascent technology takes time to evolve. It's worth referencing Engelbart's law, which is not well documented and something I learned from tech veteran David Maynard (computer scientist veteran at many startups, including Box, Digital Chocolate, and Google). Dave said, "Engelbart's law states that people's initial expectations of new technology are high—higher than can be delivered—but later performance vastly exceeds expectations." Now, if you compare this chart with Clayton Christensen's graph *The Innovator's Dilemma*,[4] you'll see that early and medium-term adopters come along disproportionately early in the life span of disruptive technology, and many BD leaders drop out of the race before the evolution occurs. The first picture below is Engelbart's law. The second picture shows Clayton Christensen's graph. The point is this: hire when you feel that your technology is about to hit the intersection, and then keep that person around until it fully matures.

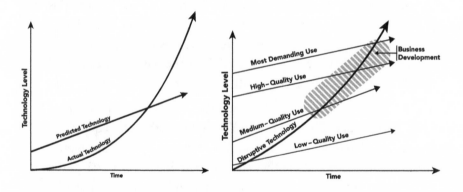

INCENT YOUR HIRE

Aligning with the graphs above, a BD hire must drive high-quality and demanding use while aligning with long-term growth that could be five to seven years away. As a result, BD hires should receive a significant sum of their compensation through equity so that it pays off with the company's success. They can also receive cash compensation based on the progress of deals and the closing of transactions. But sticking it out is a must for the company. Conversely, my recommendation for any BD executive is to make sure you are doing the right deal to make sure it's worth sticking it out.

So how do you structure the bonus plan? I like to divide it into two: half as planning and progress and the other half as performance (closed deals).

Planning and progress are a must to manage not only your internal team but also your executives. A significant amount of time should be spent internally facing and preparing the team to execute the deal. Because deals take a lot of time, you can measure and incentivize progress by looking at the number of meetings held, customer feedback, and communication with the executive team. A planning and progress bonus can be about 30 percent of the overall bonus.

The other 70 percent of the bonus is rewarded on performance. Remunerate a larger percentage of cash bonuses for closed deals based on three stages: when an agreement is signed, when the partnership goes live, and when the generation of continuous revenues occurs. You can split the bonus into halves if you choose two stages. Calculate the bonus on top-line revenues or gross margin (preferred). Margin-based commissions can range from 10–20 percent of gross margins, while revenue-based commissions are much lower (3–5 percent). Spread these out over one or two years to keep the BD representative involved with the customer over the long term. I talk more about this in the handoff section in Chapter 18.

Increase equity each year. The BD hire should want a liquidity event that is at least many times what could be made in cash. To do this, you'll want to increase equity over time, optimally every year. That way, you incent the BD Captain for making progress and sticking around until the lighthouses land. Big hitters put their money where their mouth is—in equity. Make it worth their time, and they will make it worth yours. But if they are pushing for cash, tell them to go work at Facebook or Google.

With that in mind, though, should you hire someone inside the company or reach out for external assistance?

HIRE INTERNALLY OR EXTERNALLY?

In practice, it's best to hire internally whenever possible. The BD team's involvement within your organization will likely extend to every one of your departments. Getting assistance internally is a must, especially if advocating large-scale changes to a startup's business approach is necessary. Your BD leader selects a team from the product, engineering, marketing, legal, and finance departments. This support team will attend meetings together, produce documents, or even help in the sales relationship process. More about this in Chapter 9.

Ben Horowitz disagrees. In his book *The Hard Thing about Hard Things*, he suggests asking the question, "Do I value internal or external knowledge more for this position?"[5] It may be that no one on the inside knows how to land enterprise accounts. Knowledge like how your lighthouses think, how the organization is structured, how to get to the relevant contacts, and how to set up internationally may lie outside your organization. If that's the case, then hire externally.

How Boku Made the Transition

One of the strengths and most successful aspects of Boku in its early days was that we closed deals fast. How? The internal organization moved in sync. We had a cookie-cutter contract with variable terms, discussed and agreed on by our head lawyer. I could negotiate those terms at will, but anything outside of that needed his approval. Finance also had an approved, delimited standard fee structure. Marketing buttressed the sales team with research and presentation materials, so salespeople had ready-to-go presentations. We had a product person who acted as sales engineer and two people on the customer success team. Salespeople ("hunters") offloaded deals to customer service ("farmers") so salespeople could focus on hunting. That company structure allowed us to scale efficiently and effectively.

Once we'd done that, we were able to add a BD role to level up. Leveling up required everyone to step up. We had to generate interest in our product at an enterprise level, build secure and robust technology, and create a global footprint that could access billions of people—yes, if you want to do a deal with Apple, you'd better reach a billion customers. We invested ample resources into the product, our presentation materials and theatricals, and our travel budget. Sales cycles got longer, and we touched many more people at these technology behemoths. All in all, leveling up was fun, and we learned a lot, too.

We also had to play more sophisticated games—almost on par with investment bankers. In sales, people may buy your product based on a relationship, a coolness, a friend's recommendation, or someone who takes you to posh restaurants—or, in our case, played the same video games. In BD, this *never* happens. The people on the other side are highly educated lawyers, bankers, or consultants, with a very keen eye on their terms of the deal and return on investment—that's it. They care about your competitive advantages, not about your network of friends. They care more about how your company will add value and innovate over time and less about what you are hawking today. They will dive into your models and spreadsheets to make sure your assumptions are correct, not waste time wine tasting with you. They have bosses educated at business and law schools, not new-money, freewheeling entrepreneurs.

How did we do it? *We methodically executed deals.* By working closely with our target companies to help them fully understand the market, we leapfrogged the competition. This work entailed country-by-country analysis with spreadsheets, market forecasting models, and global research. We created detailed mock-ups and flows and demonstrated our product flexibility. To help the lighthouse get internal approval, we created examples of RFPs and wrote up documents. At the end of all this, we designed an in-depth presentation (with 100+ slides) and delivered it to dozens of team members on the prospective buyers' corporate development, product, engineering, marketing, legal, and finance teams. That's the kind of holistic, in-sync teamwork you need if you want to get the attention of your lighthouse deal, reel them in, and not just cross the chasm but leap over it.

Please note: I often use the term "sales" in this book to denote the act of selling, the act that a BD person is fundamentally doing. In lieu of saying business developing, I just say selling or salesperson, and so forth.

CHAPTER 2

KNOW THE LIGHTHOUSE FRAMEWORK

"I tend to work from a physics framework. And physics teaches you to reason from first principles rather than by analogy."

—Elon Musk[6]

A great mariner looks to the stars to chart his course as a guide through the stormy waters. Likewise, when we stepped back and saw the chasm approaching at Boku, we pulled out the maps and compasses to guide us, looking for new land. Our junior sales team spent about a month researching over 300 potential targets. We brainstormed every market—mobile games, music, magazines/periodicals, dating websites, mobile purchases that didn't use in-app billing, e-commerce, TV, parking applications, highway toll booths, and more.

This research and analysis led us to meetings and deals with companies of all sorts. Because we were so persuasive and stubborn, we'd get meetings and some deals, but none worked out financially. All wasn't lost, though. The trial-and-error partnerships provided us with technology and a stepping-stone to prepare us for the lighthouse accounts. We learned from the partnerships, gained a step up against the competition, and achieved a market perception as the leading innovator. Although we didn't know it at the time, we were positioned to capture the ensuing lighthouse deals.

That's the point of the lighthouse framework. It guides you to unseen directions that you didn't think were tenable. If you keep the path steady, even when the winds blow strong, you'll make it through. After all, the lighthouse is just a guiding light.

To find the guiding light, learn the lighthouse framework below.

Where to Start?

The most common scenario at the beginning of any BD project goes as follows: you think one of several transformational deals is possible yet still can't figure out how to go about it. You're at a loss when it comes to figuring out which accounts are the right ones for you to pursue. Then when you do, the questions linger:

- Should you approach these targets immediately or wait?
- Can you get to the right person at the target account?
- Is it worth all the investment and time?
- Even if you close the deal, will they demand so much that it takes all of your resources?

These thoughts go round and round. It's a conundrum and feels like a no-win scenario. No CEO in their right mind would throw the kitchen sink at one or two glimmers of hope.

Or would they?

They would if they calculate the expected probability of getting that lighthouse deal. A believable lighthouse analysis could attract investors and affect the valuation materially. One of BD's main objectives is to scale the company over time—so much so that new investors may want to jump aboard. It's BD's job to change things up and add exponential growth through groundbreaking deals. *That's* why it's critical to separate deals into categories that make sense for sales and BD functions.

The Lighthouse Framework

The lighthouse framework will help you to organize and analyze your pipeline. It serves as a map to your lighthouse that will help you determine product interest well before finding the right fit. Eventually, you'll divide your deals into two or three categories so you know who will be chasing what. Let's get into the weeds.

ORGANIZING THE DEAL PIPELINE

Brainstorm. Brainstorming is one of my favorite activities in life—just paint a bunch of ideas on a wall with no wrong answer. Similarly, create an exhaustive, theoretical pipeline for your company with ideas that range from the strangest deal to the dream deal, and then throw those potentials into a spreadsheet. This spreadsheet is the beginning of your search for your startup's lighthouse account.

There's nothing better for visualizing your options than a detailed spreadsheet, no matter how old-school it seems to make one. Your lighthouse analysis framework—the mechanism you use to keep track of all your potential lighthouse companies—will center on this one spreadsheet. Think of the framework as a statistical equation. Can you figure out the most statistically significant variable? (With a background in econometrics, that's the framework I use to distill information.) You're trying to figure out where the market is going and what the most attractive opportunities are. If BD's movement toward a lighthouse account is a journey, then this spreadsheet is your map. The better your calculations, the more efficiently you navigate.

The first step is to do a market and vertical analysis. Say you want to look at the possibility of grocery stores adopting your technologies and how big that opportunity may be. Then you'd need to do some work to figure out the size of the opportunities that you are targeting. Do your work by combing through 10-Ks and other financial information either online or through your network. In this framework, you must ensure your data is correct. Get data from employers, past employees, customers, future customers, and whoever will give you an idea about the prospects. In the next few chapters, I'll discuss how to get data from the market. Good inputs equal good outputs.

Here are a few variables to consider when doing a market or vertical analysis:

1. **Size**—Vertical market size by revenue broken down into revenue per prospect. Estimate the repeatability of selling the same product to many customers.

2. **Growth**—The growth rate of the market.

3. **Market concentration**—The more competition or fragmentation in a market, the more opportunities to sign a deal because those companies will adopt new technology to get a leg up on the others.

4. **Outsource versus insource**—The likelihood that existing companies will develop the technology in-house.

5. **Rate of adoption**—Have they adopted new technologies quickly before? What's their impetus to have done so?

That analysis will give you an idea which verticals will fit your product. Now let's look at company-specific variables. With the help of enterprise sales veteran Richard Purcell, we derived the following set of variables.

Let's look at the target company's interests.

1. **Revenue**—The revenue potential for the target company as a function of the partnership. How much can they make from it?

2. **Strategic**—Strategic interest in startup's specific technology— i.e., how badly do they need new technologies to protect their golden egg?

3. **Adoption curve**—Speed to adopt new technologies. (Is the industry fast-moving?)

4. **Preparation**—Are they structured/prepared to do a deal? Do they have a qualified person in charge, like a chief digital officer for a brick-and-mortar chain?

5. **Requirements**—Do they have lots of requirements to adopt new technology such as custom features or development? (More custom work = less appealing.)

Your company's (the startup's) interests:

1. **Revenue**—What is the revenue potential for your company?

2. **Monetary cost**—How much is the product development investment required to win the deal?

3. **Opportunity cost**—How much time might be involved to pursue each target at the expense of a different opportunity?

4. **Contact**—How strong is your contact? Were you introduced via a warm intro or a cold call?

5. **Strategic**—How strategic is that company in terms of winning other deals?

There may be other variables, but these are a good start. Using a basic 1–5 rating will quantify the variables. Overall, your spreadsheet should have eight to ten variables. Applying weighted average percentages per variable, you can roughly equate which deals may offer the highest expected value, and thus, it may be wise to spend time on them.

Pipeline Analysis

Scan the QR code to view this
information as a spreadsheet.

The goal of this analysis is to prioritize the deals that will most likely get you into the "money flow" and take a meat ax to the others. The money flow is where there is an imminent need for the product with a large potential user base. The money flow equation is simple: lots of money = high need + large and engaged existing user/employee base + price. Optimize those three variables and that's either a lighthouse or transformative deal.

When the analysis is complete, you will have ten or so potential lighthouse deals. Stephen Lee, former VP of Treasure Data (acquired by Softbank) turned venture capitalist, suggests, "One way I like to look at Tier 1 partnerships is to pick no more than five companies so you don't put all your eggs in one basket; you spend 75 percent of your time on those—building out account plans and defining in great detail the success criteria. There may be another five or ten deals you keep warm, pinging them and having occasional conversations, just in case one of them unexpectedly jumps to the top."

What your initial discussions will reveal is that you'll have to make tradeoffs to get a deal. When looking over your list of potential accounts, you will face the difficulty of comparing apples with oranges—the quantitative (the expected revenue and costs) with the qualitative variables (the impact on your future by having a big-name account). In some cases, impactful is going to mean revenue. *Not always the case for a lighthouse*: a big reason why lighthouse deals are a key strategy is what the deal means for the broader market. You may need to win the lighthouse at any cost under the assumption that profits will come later. This kind of lighthouse account acts as a signal to the market of your company's leadership and technical ability and makes the path to obtaining even bigger deals much clearer.

Create a Tier Sales Structure

Tier 3 Deals	Tier 2 Deals	Tier 1 Deals
Low-Hanging Fruit	Stepping Stones	Lighthouse Deals
+ 1-3 month lead time + 1-on-1 sales + Standard deal terms	+ 6-12 month lead time + 2-3 person deal team + Custom deal terms	+ 12+ month lead time + 5-6 person deal team + Custom terms & product features
	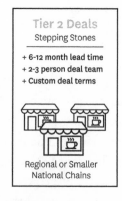	
Local Coffee Shop (1000s of them)	Regional or Smaller National Chains	Large National or Worldwide Brands

In addition, the analysis may uncover certain dependencies to get deals done. These are stepping-stone deals. For example, even though Deal X may be the largest revenue generator, it may take a long time to execute. Furthermore, Deal X may not move until Deal W is complete. And Deal Y—which is revenue accretive—will take about the same time as W, but W wants a costly custom feature. You really want X, so which one do you chase? That's for you to decide with the analysis. Over time, you can fine-tune your equation to account for such factors and decide which ones are stepping-stones to the lighthouse.

Upon completion of the analysis, the spreadsheet will spit out different tiers of deals. From there, it's easy to divide them up between different members of your GTM team.

Life isn't a spreadsheet or Salesforce, though. In Chapter 5, you will set out to stormy seas, and as you reach out to companies, you will learn whether your assumptions were correct. Adjust your priorities accordingly as you proceed, and stay flexible. There are new CRM tools that can help you with this tracking, like Gong and Scratchpad, so it's worth comparing these with rudimentary spreadsheets. Manage your time based on the likelihood the deal will progress. This also becomes important later in the negotiation phase. It's likely your company can support only one or two of these deals so you will have negotiating power if you can get two to the finish line.

Startup veteran and consultant Richard Purcell sums it all up. He stresses that doing quantitative and qualitative research is critical before you go to market. It needs to be continually measured because most startups never find product-market fit. Further, others don't find a repeatable market to sell into. Start by doing your analysis, find a need for your product, and sell it over and over.

BOKU'S OUTCOME OF ANALYSIS: IDENTIFYING THE LIGHTHOUSES

In the chapter introduction, I mentioned that we analyzed over 300 deals and pursued several different markets while simultaneously chasing deals with Apple, Google, Microsoft, and Sony. Although we quickly realized what the transformational deals could be, we couldn't foresee which ones were lighthouses. By pursuing stepping-stone deals that helped with product development or geographic expansion, we figured out which of the mega deals would move first and become the lighthouse.

The CEO of Boku, Jon Prideaux, oversaw several of these exercises. "Be aware of analysis paralysis," he warns. "If you want to land a lighthouse, the spreadsheet doesn't need to extend to hundreds of rows to find them. But the analysis and working on stepping-stone deals can help you figure out what to do and how to get there more efficiently. At some point, you need to take risks and try out some of these partnerships, regardless of revenue generation."

To his point, not all deals will work out in terms of revenue. For example, we attempted a few trial deals in smart TVs, parking, and magazines, which enhanced our product development. Although most of these scenarios didn't pan out in huge financial gains, we earned invaluable knowledge about the limitations and opportunities for our payment technology. That knowledge came in handy when pitching to the large tech companies, proving our creativity and technical flexibility. It was the Sony deal that eventually served as our lighthouse—providing both revenues and product development—and signaled to Microsoft and Apple we were indeed the player to be reckoned with.

The key outcome of the lighthouse framework is to decide which deals are worth chasing, then which ones to invest in once you catch them—hopefully on the way to the lighthouse.

CHAPTER 3

BUSINESS DEVELOPMENT AS A STRATEGIC WEAPON

"Several Japanese firms were made to employ clerks who had no other work than to obtain information for the Japanese authorities…Spies were employees of Takenokohsi Trading Company, Daido Boeki, and Mitsui Bussan Kaisha."

—In the 1940s, the Official East Indies Netherlands Government wrote a report called *Ten Years of Japanese Burrowing in the Netherlands East Indies*[7]

Long ago, the *sogo shosha*—Japanese trading firms—derived their information-collecting techniques from the Japanese military and spies. Nearly 80 years later, these trading firms still flourish—even when many academics, business theorists, and doubters of the trading firms said the middleman would be cut out. By diligently researching, investigating, and placing bets on each new global opportunity, not only have they avoided being cut out, but they've also thrived. I learned these strategic tactics when I worked at Mitsui Bussan, one of the largest trading firms in Japan.

Strategy is overrated—at least in a traditional sense where people read research papers, sit around a room, and draw on a whiteboard. That process won't work, and you should certainly not pay some chief strategy officer to do that. There are now startups all over the world competing against you. The strategy is simple: the best product and the most market share wins. Beware: a causal relationship it isn't. Fast movers can win a market with an inferior product to competitors. To win, you need to iterate your product set while winning market share, commensurately.

To do this, thoroughly understand the levers of those two variables, then prioritize which ones to pull. Strategy with no priorities equals hope, and hope isn't a plan.

Don't let your ship get tossed about. You know where to find the lighthouses. Now jibe and tack to get there. When to jibe and tack is the strategy; the how are the tactics.

Start by leading in market intelligence at the planning level. Market intelligence can help you understand the market dynamics and what you need to do to develop a comparative advantage. With the correct critical thinking, a business developer—through many discussions—can iterate, chart your course, and execute the strategy.

Lead in Market Intelligence

Gathering and retaining information is a competitive advantage that many don't consider. Furthermore, the market moves, and it's important to know how long your product advantages may last. Your goal is to figure out what moves to make and how fast to make them. To gauge this, you'll need the market intelligence and research skills of a CIA operative.

GAIN MARKET INTELLIGENCE: KNOW THE BARKING

First, to lead in market intelligence, you must attain market information and decipher what it's telling you. How do you do this? As Jon Prideaux would say, "Understand the barking dogs within your company." Interpret what you see, hear, and feel from each of your teams.

Dogs That Don't Bark: Internal Research

Your product and marketing groups are the dogs that don't usually bark. They keep their heads down, working, researching, and developing creative directions to lead the company. Steve Jobs said, "People don't know what they want until you show it to them...Our task is to read things that are not yet on the page." A good product manager can figure out what to write on the page. For this reason, if your product and marketing teams are making a racket, listen.

Dogs That Bark: External Feedback

Sales and customer success teams are the two dogs that bark. The dogs that bark most reliably are the customer success teams. This group implements direct feedback from customers in an organized manner to keep existing clients and bring on more. Because this group has customers on hand, prioritize them the most. The most valuable customers are the ones you have.

The dogs that bark less reliably are the sales teams. This group spends most of their time speaking to customers off-the-cuff and often has *too* many ideas. To winnow down these ideas, your sales group should organize feature sets with the number of requests and details about each. Send this prioritized list to a marketing or product member who can analyze data from customer success and sales teams.

Dogs That Howl at the Moon: Dreamer's Feedback

A colleague of mine once called me a dreamer. I replied that I was a dream chaser. If I weren't, he wouldn't be rich. BD people like me are the dogs who howl at the moon. To those inside the company, our howls may seem obnoxious, but a good BD person will move on from a botched deal to an incredible one with equal persistence and energy.

Treat these three dog packs as the inputs for your company's output. Depending on the context, sometimes you'll need to put more weight in some packs than others. Over time, your existing customer set, the visionaries, will become less significant. As a result, you'll need to dedicate fewer resources to implementing customer feedback. Conversely, when you get to the edge of the chasm, you'll need to put more weight on the howls of BD. After all, their moonshots are your company's greatest hope for jumping on a unicorn and catching the attention of a lighthouse.

RECONCILE FEEDBACK AND MAKE A WAKE FAST

So what do you do with all these barking dogs? Answer: reconcile the feedback. With this intelligence, you need to move quickly to implement the strategy that makes you stand out. When you start to assess your product's strengths and weaknesses, you'll discover that what *you* think are your advantages are not always what your existing customers or potential customers think. Existing customers tell you how you compare against the scuttlebutt; further, they tell you where you are lacking but how you compensate for your shortcomings—trying to be courteous. Potential customers tell you what the differences are that they've gathered through hearsay and what they've bought into. Product advantages are often indecipherable unless a vendor compares them side by side—which few ever do. Then what?

Reconcile feedback from the barking dogs. Figure out what part of the product is an advantage and what gossip prevails. Make sure your potential lighthouse knows the facts, either through customer referrals or testing the product. Also, be honest about any weaknesses, and let them know that if they need those features, they are coming. Figure out the discrepancies, then move fast.

Be the boat that makes the wake. The market is constantly in flux. You want to be seen as the fastest mover and market leader. To do that, you'll need to forecast how your advantages will help you stay ahead of the competition. It doesn't happen overnight; it takes many iterations of product improvements and market positioning attempts. Keep making the waves that throw the others off their anchor.

Any advantage is a function of time, so ask yourself a few questions. If you are trailing a competitor, how long will it take to oust them from a certain client—that is, the sales cycle? If you want to gain that client, what product features need to be developed, and can you do it more quickly than your competitor? What's the probability of success? To retain a client, should you develop a new product feature X? How much of an advantage will it give you if you do so? For how long? These are just a few questions to gauge whether time is on your side.

BOKU'S EVOLUTION

Here is an example of how Boku evolved in three phases over almost a decade. In phase one, we broke into the market with a simple-to-integrate, mass-market, and relatively undifferentiated product. In phase two, we progressed to a slightly differentiated, higher-cost-than-market product that was global in scale with a standard feature set. This phase occurred after an acquisition gave us clear competitive advantages in terms of product pricing, tech capabilities, and global coverage. There, we hit the chasm. To cross the chasm in phase three, we advanced to a highly customizable, international product that was focused on large-scale clients with lower-per-transaction pricing. We built a seamless technology that only the most notable accounts could use and customize as needed. We narrowed our client set in phase two and again in phase three, focusing only on our lighthouse accounts. In the end, winning those accounts gave us product advantages and disproportionate scale over our competitors. Companies and products evolve. You want to be the one evolving the fastest.

By the end, we made waves in the market; we didn't get tossed about and let others do it. We jibed and tacked, creating our own evolution and course to the lighthouse.

UNDERSTAND MARKET DYNAMICS

You know how you fare against the other ships at sea. Each ship has a beachhead on different islands, making it tough to oust them. If you are lucky, you'll find a deserted island. The journey there exposes you to other risks. These are the market dynamics that you must consider before setting sail.

KNOW THE TYPES OF SEAS—THAT IS, MARKET SCENARIOS

Generally, there are three market scenarios: (1) greenfield, (2) incremental value-add, and (3) displacement. Every company dreams of being the first in a greenfield market. When Slack replaced company email and DocuSign replaced hand signatures, those were greenfield opportunities—completely untapped markets with little to no competition. In those cases, do all that you can to win market share. If you are adding incremental value, you will play in a more defined niche—that also means a smaller market size. This is where most startups like Boku fall. In the third case, if you are trying to displace a legacy product, you must offer a far superior product at a price that is on par or better than that of incumbents. That's very difficult for a startup. Identify the market you are entering and the competitor's stronghold before you move into new waters.

What Kind of Market?

| 1. **Immense Greenfield Opportunities** | 2. **Your Service Offers Add-ons of Incremental Value** | 3. **Unseat Existing Market to Require Switching** |

BEWARE OF THE RISKS AT SEA

It's worth expounding on ancillary market risks when thinking about the moves you are about to make. Risk management is a key to any business decision making. So know the risks at hand.

Beware of an Identity Crisis

Don't try to do too much; pick one or two paths and focus on execution. Many startups get confused because they try to be everything to everyone. For example, either be a low-cost provider with easy onboarding or a high-value-add provider with white-glove customer service. That means pick a customer segment in one industry or a company size that will reap the most value from your product.

Beware of Your Competitors' Movements

Know what your competitors are doing. Find out as much information about what they are doing as possible. If they are funded more than you and moving faster, how will you fend them off? In which direction might they be headed? Map these scenarios out in a SWOT diagram that shows today and predicts one year from now. How will you fit in?

Beware of Markets with Deeply Entrenched Competitors

No matter how good your product may be, it's nearly impossible to wedge out an entrenched competitor. For your counterpart to risk their job and do a deal with you, you'll need a better technology, lower risk, and lower price. A colleague once told me, "You can have two of three advantages: better, faster, and cheaper. But you can't get all three."

Beware of Markets with Lots of Regulation

Governments regulate many markets, including taxis, hotels, payments, security, and more. Although they are notoriously slow, just be aware of the risks that may affect your ability to scale. Many companies go full force to break the system, resulting in a remake of regulation. That's a win if you can do it.

Beware of Markets That Are Smaller than Anticipated or Don't Evolve

Sometimes markets don't develop fast enough or at all. Monitor when the market will turn in your favor and hit the inflection curve. If the tides do not turn, your BD team should devise escape plans. Even a great management team won't succeed in a small market.

Use BD to Maneuver through Turbulent Seas

Now that you've familiarized yourself with the different markets, have an idea of the competitive landscape, and have identified risks, it's time to chart your course and maneuver your ship. Once you do that, you can execute. This section is the how—the jibe and tacking—across the chasm.

CHART YOUR COURSE

With the understanding of your position in relation to your competitors', it's time to chart a course to the lighthouse. As you look across the chasm, a few thoughts may cross your mind. Should you stay the course until the market moves your way? Should you adjust your strategy or change it completely? Should you buy up competitors in your market?

Any way you go, you must enhance your product, pricing, and perception. Let's run through each of these options.

There is nothing wrong with staying the course if your balance sheet can support you. However, not making a move to change your market position is a risky proposition long term. Without a plan, your venture-capital-funded opponents will have throttled into high gear and left you behind in a rowboat before you know it. Being the change maker is always better than being the recipient of unwelcome change.

Tweaking your trajectory will involve leveraging the key assets of your business to enter a slightly tangential market. Leverage core assets—I cannot stress this enough. Your people, knowledge, relationships, and technology are all assets that you've financially and emotionally established. Use them. Can your existing business relationships be utilized to help both of you move into a new market that neither of you are currently in? Can you build new technology on top of what you've done already and move into a new sector? Can you slightly change the focus or customer you are working with? Although that may seem minor, the lens through which you look at your business often needs adjustment—just flip it to the next degree. After I left Boku, the company utilized its mobile phone carrier relationships and tapped a new market in identity solutions—in addition to payments. A small tweak may yield a greater-than-expected return.

A big tweak, or a pivot, usually doesn't, however. Pivoting means doing something drastically different in hopes of addressing a much larger opportunity. In essence, you are starting again by building off a base product to tap into an alternative market, completely new seas. I've seen this happen many times in Silicon Valley. More often than not, you are likely to fail. New technology and business relationships will be time consuming to reestablish. Keep in mind that as a new player in that industry, clients will want to know what happened to your other business and where you suddenly got the license to play. Often, you won't have it, so you need to make sure the change you propose is near fail-safe, with no risk. That's hard to do, and so is pivoting.

Don't pivot until you've tried everything to tap your initial market. Boku tried when it attempted a move into mobile wallets, nearly bankrupting the company. Although that team tried to leverage an existing customer base (albeit a very different department in the same corporation), the technology and user acquisition was immensely different from our existing path; it drained most of our resources from the standing mobile payments business. Even though the mobile payments business was unstable—not shipwrecked—our executive team ignored the seas we were in and looked elsewhere. By all means, try to win the market you are in before looking for new ones. But if you're bailing out water from your ship, a pivot may be the only path forward.

After that near-fatal decision, Boku's strategy shifted back to the existing business and embarked on an acquisitive strategy, buying up its opponents—thanks to my drum beating. Although it can be brutal, it's an efficient way to cross. This strategy particularly works if all competitors are in a stalemate hitting the chasm. If that's happening, you may be receiving some inquiries about joining forces. All companies will realize that the day has come to join forces rather than beat each other up in a small market. You want to end up as the last ship standing, not the also-ran. So when that happens, it may be an excellent time to consult your investors and consider such a strategy. I'll elaborate more on this in Chapter 8.

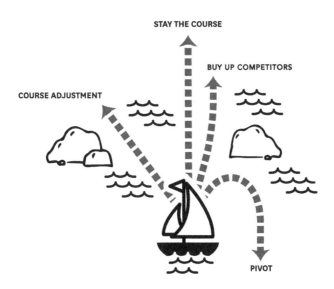

EXECUTE THE COURSE

After you've picked your direction, don't look back. Execute the course. How do you do this? Through different types of BD deals, you can solidify your product advantages or shore up your market presence and positioning.

Speed Kills: Get to Lighthouse Accounts Quickly and Establish Market Presence

Get to these groundbreaking deals quickly. Be the first to approach them and get on the top of their lists. The first one in will be seen as a market leader/innovator.

Speed Kills, Again: Grab Market Share to Grow Market Presence

Get your product into the hands of customers quickly with a freemium version or a self-serve option. (I'll elaborate more in Chapter 12.) Once the product is in the customer's hands, you'll be able to attain information to create a proper strategy. The bigger the deal, the more prolonged the sales cycles. Shorten that sales cycle, and you'll move faster than the competition.

Structure Exclusive Deals to Secure Market Presence

Structure an exclusive deal that signals to the market: your product is untouchable. It may be costly and unprofitable initially, but it may reap handsome returns down the road. At Boku, we did an exclusive deal with one of the three social games companies at the time called Playfish (which later sold to EA). Due to the terms, the deal didn't make money, but it sent a message to Facebook that we outperformed our competitor, wielding them to work with us.

Fundraise Faster to Monopolize the Market

In 2021, Silicon Valley companies raised over $100 million in less than a year. Startups are making this a core advantage to deter would-be contenders. Whether international expansion or corporate development, the company will need capital. In fact, a rich balance sheet can be a competitive advantage to outlast market downturns as well as buy up competitors. Trust me, I still remember when Boku's founder Mark Britto would half-jokingly quip, "Raising capital and writing RFPs are our competitive advantages."

Expand Internationally to Create a Global Market Presence

Show the market that you are ready to handle deals that stretch across the globe. Trillion-dollar companies need partners that can expand globally. It may be time to dip your toe in the water and hire consultants or set up offices internationally. It's relatively easy to do with a small investment. The goal is to gather market information locally, expand current customers in other countries, or start selling directly.

Coinvest in Product Development

Tweak your product by investing together with customers. Doing deals that require investment will build your product knowledge and intellectual property—assuming that you retain it. Choose these deals carefully with the lighthouse account in mind. If they need it, go in the red and do it. (Even better if you can get the customer to pay for it.)

Pedagogically, Prepare Marketing Materials

This point may sound trivial, but it's not. Prepare your research, presentations, and turnaround materials efficiently. That takes teamwork from marketing and other parts of the organization. Over time, if you stay organized, the turnaround times will quicken. The more professional and prepared you are, the more the lighthouse accounts will respect you. Always follow up within two days of your last meeting.

Expedite Product Development and Market Presence through Corporate Development

Corporate development can fill gaps. One way to grab market share is by acquiring competitors who have a portion of the market. Buy them to buy their customers. With practice, corporate development can be a competitive advantage. More about this in Chapter 8.

How Boku Used BD to Gain a Strategic Advantage

At Boku, to cross the chasm from the marketplace of virtual goods (which include social games companies like Zynga) to the digital goods markets (like Apple and Google), we demonstrated the best product and market leadership perception. We listened to the market, created a global advantage, and executed it.

The reliable dogs tipped us off first. Our first tip came from Nicholas Reidy, our VP of Customer Success, who said that Boku's existing customers were requesting that we lower our fees on par with or lower than prepaid cards, and if we could do that, they'd increase our payment volume. Prepaid or so-called gift cards were found—and are still found today—at any shopping market or convenience store checkout line. He worked closely with the product team to analyze this market structure. Our CS team focused our sights on a bigger competitor than the immediate ones in our ship's purview.

But our cost was still questionable. We kept digging. By talking to others in the industry, we discovered that the fees on gift cards ranged from 12–20 percent. Gift card providers had to pay fees to their vendors. Likewise, we were paying even higher costs to mobile phone carriers. That was the aha moment. If we could get our carrier fees down to the same rate that gift card providers paid their vendors, we could shake up the market. After all, we had a better user experience. In this way, we also realized that our competitors weren't other carrier billing companies but prepaid card companies. We zoomed our sights to a new market, but our costs were still iffy.

With this research, our mobile phone carrier sales team went to the carriers and pitched our plan to bring down fees. Our GM in Europe, James Patmore, and his team concocted the VIP Program, targeting the most proliferate telecoms who'd be interested in working with our potential merchants. He hypothesized that if the carriers received more payment volume and connected with top-brand merchants, they may be willing to lower their fees. Telecoms would do anything to align with major brands—like Apple, Google, Facebook, and Sony—who initially wanted to steer clear of the telecom carriers. Telecoms also told us we'd need to implement new technology, which mirrored that of credit card processing. We invested in that technology and secured the carriers as entrusted partners.

That gave us global coverage, a technical superiority, and price parity with a competitive solution (already in use). In the end, we got a handful of carriers to commit around the world; that excited our lighthouses and pushed them forward. This example also accentuates team sales, whereby teams in different geographies work together to get deals done, which I'll discuss in Chapter 9.

To win these deals, we gathered information from dogs that bark and dogs that don't bark, then executed a global strategy to catch our lighthouse accounts. That strategy was threefold: fees on par with or below prepaid cards, specifically targeted global coverage, and seamless technology to interface with their platforms. Get your product and price right and then lead market presence, and you will be the last one at sea.

CHAPTER 4

THE MOST BELIEVABLE STORY WINS

"Your story was almost too good; we kept looking for something wrong with it."

—A payments executive

This comment is hardly a compliment; I would've been disappointed if the story had been anything less than airtight. My team and I knew that a company's story makes or breaks a business plan, so we worked on refining it from the very start.

Our story was concise: we had the technology that provided the best customer experience, the broadest global coverage, a price on par with or better than other existing solutions, and a proven track record of servicing large clients. That's a simple story to tell, albeit a demanding one to carry out. Like ours, your product's story should be simple and persuasive. Most people don't remember more than two points after a meeting, so really home in on what sets you apart, and don't worry if the lighthouse doesn't remember everything. Do you know what's even more succinct than that? Tell them what to remember.

This chapter is the nitty-gritty—that is, the essentials—of BD. How you tell your story sets the tone for the entire relationship with your lighthouse account and the market. To get a story as tight as ours was, you'll need to take all that you learned about strategy in the last chapter and turn it into a story of unique value propositions and differentiators. What sets you apart? Why should the lighthouse place stock in you over your competitors? Learn this now because it's the foundation of more to come.

Here are the steps to do this: build out a detailed slide deck with three use cases, transpose it into a natural dialogue, and nail down a defensible position. The one who tells the most believable story wins.

Prepare Three Types of Deliveries

There are generally three occasions during which you'll have to "tell your company's story"—the standard sales deck, the elevator or cocktail party pitch, and the deep-dive presentation. Master these three deliveries in the BD context, and you will be good to go.

The Three Pitch Types

Elevator/Cocktail Party	Standard Sales Pitch	Deep Dive Presentation
+ 1-2 minutes	+ 30 minutes	+ For sophisticated, larger clients who want detail
+ Communicate your distinct advantage	+ Slide deck presentation	+ Prepared especially for specific clients
+ Five-word hook plus open-ended question	+ Remember custom slide for company X	+ Up to 100 slides in a deck
+ Memorizable and repeatable by your whole team	+ Be prepared for Q&A after	+ May contain confidential information
	+ Foundation of your master slide deck	

THE NARRATION: THE STANDARD SALES DECK

Start with a standard intro pitch that highlights your strengths. When creating your slide deck, several factors will set you apart. First, the overview of the team, vision, and solution prove why you are the most credible partner. This is your lede. Second, the depth of your knowledge about the market and how you differentiate is your most compelling selling point. And last, the effort you put into tailoring your presentation to their specific company will set you apart.

This slide deck should be the basic setup for any first meeting that lasts thirty minutes with a Q&A. With a few alterations, your presentation should follow this basic flow:

1. **Company overview**—Create credibility and let them know why they should listen to you.

2. **Company vision**—What's your mission and vision?

3. **Problem**—What's the problem you're solving, how big is it, and how does it relate to the customer's problem?

4. **Product/Solution**—What's your solution, and what are your product features and future roadmap?

5. **Market analysis**—What is the size of the market and who are the competitors? What approach do they take to solve the problem?

6. **Competitors/Competitive advantages**—How do you fare versus the competition? What don't they get, and what makes you better? (Leave this out in the written presentations due to legal risks.)

7. **Custom slides for company X**—What can you do for the lighthouse account you're courting? How does your product fit in with their current offering?

8. **Business model**—Don't give pricing but general money flows. Sales can lead with a price, but BD shouldn't. The wrong number up front may get you a big whammy when they shut down the conversation immediately. Hold that for ensuing discussions. You want to be the partner of choice, not the price of choice.

9. **Why now?**—What's the urgency? Is their golden egg at risk? Will a competitor adopt this technology faster than they will?

10. **Why you?**—More of question 6.

11. **Customer testimonials**—Let others praise you.

What's the sign of a good pitch deck? It's when the customer's mind is in sync with yours—almost like extrasensory perception. If, during a presentation, for example, your next slide answers the question the lighthouse just asked, you are in sync. There are few answers more powerful than saying, "I've got your answer on the next slide." If you can get the lighthouse on your wavelength, that's a good sign.

Note that there may be a "Version 2" of the standard deck to leave with clients. Often, clients will ask for the presented slide deck, with a bit of added information, so it's wise to have a presentation pitch deck and a leave-behind pitch deck with more detailed info. A live presentation usually has one or two points per slide, whereas a leave-behind may have two or three with detailed descriptions. Update your "Version 2" after the meeting and send it to them. Remember, limit your turnarounds to a few days.

THE ELEVATOR OR COCKTAIL PARTY PITCH

Some call it the elevator pitch. I prefer the cocktail party pitch. Why? I've never pitched to anyone in an elevator, and that sounds formal and stuffy, but I've pitched to a lot of people over cocktails. This one- to two-minute story should only come out in informal settings when you're networking and trying to get that initial contact—done better with a martini in hand. Did I mention, lychee, please?

A five-word hook plus an open-ended question like "What do you think?" is your go-to entry point. Any time-constrained executive won't want to hear more than those five words. If your five words work, you'll get the space for the one or two sentences needed to generate more interest. A good cocktail party speech will include your startup's competitive advantage, a glimpse of the future, and most likely, a happy customer anecdote. Your short cocktail party pitch isn't going to get any deals done, but it will get you the leads you need.

An example of this was when I was traversing the conference floor in Germany at Gamescom in 2009. I just happened to sit down next to Riccardo Zacconi, the CEO of King.com. Our conversation went something like this:

"Hi! I'm Kurt from Boku, also an Index Ventures portfolio company. We do carrier billing and would like to work with you. Do you have a few minutes?" (By the way, using a mutual connection, especially an investor, is helpful.)

"Hi, Kurt. Sorry, I'm off to my next meeting. Carrier billing is a busy space, and we already have partners. What is your advantage?" Riccardo went right to the point.

"We connect to more countries than any other provider, and in key countries, we connect directly with carriers so we can offer better pricing and higher price points for users to pay," I replied.

He looked intrigued. "Sounds interesting. Give me your card, and I'll connect you to the right folks. Sorry, I must be off."

In less than a minute, I told him exactly what we did and our distinct advantages. He took my card, and by the end of the day, I was in contact with the right people to drive the deal forward. If you're intentional with your cocktail pitches, your company will have significantly more leads.

The cocktail pitch isn't only for you. It's also for your colleagues and customers, who in turn tell others what your company does. *That's how simple and casual it should be.* Make it so simple that your entire company can memorize this short speech and share it in the same way. You would be amazed at how successful others can be at generating leads when you've got a consistent message. Especially in tightly knit places like Silicon Valley, when your colleagues connect with friends who work at prospective companies, you'll need their support.

THE DEEP DIVE

The more sophisticated the company, the more polished your peers will be—meaning you need to turn in A+ work. Deep-dive presentations are requisite for transformational deals. The buyers' job is to make convincing and substantiated arguments to their bosses that a deal with you will benefit their company. It's your job to make sure they have the information they need to make the case.

With that in mind, the deep-dive deck must contain sufficient depth for each section. Product slides focus on market sizing, product differentiation, and integration. Engineering slides discuss technology, integration, scalability, and security. Finance slides cover payments and accounting. Legal slides talk about the compliance, product, operational quirks, and risks at play. Preparing ahead also saves time in the case of a request for proposal (RFP) that comes out of nowhere. It happens, so draw it up in advance; it will save you time and headaches. Deep-dive pitches can include as many as 100 slides and contain much confidential information, so keep it secure and only send it out to the most trusted clients. (Better yet, never send it out; just present it with your team.) A deep-dive deck is done with deep thought.

On top of the deep-dive deck, keep a master deck. The current master should be available to anyone who needs it: sales, BD, marketing, and customer success teams can grab and go. This deck ensures everyone will tell the same story and, more importantly, optimize output.

The Dialogue: A Good Story Is a Conversation

Storytelling needs to come across as unrehearsed, but to deliver a story naturally, you'll need to perfect its many moving parts. Splitting the story up does wonders, and once you've practiced it, you're set for game time.

Your pitch should never be a "hard sell." Formulaic stories full of false praise for potential customers are going to get metaphorical doors slammed in your face. Glengarry Glen Ross's *Always Be Closing* won't work. The veteran players in the business have sat through the same sales tricks thousands of times, and any particularly harsh tactics just won't work. However, by telling your company's story, you're not imposing but poking around for compatibility between you and your prospect. I can't repeat it enough: treat it like a conversation.

To help you, create a presentation that balances your pitch with your customer's business situation. Your entire pitch shouldn't be just about your solution, advantages, and future. It should also include slides that bring up potential problems your customer faces and synergistic scenarios between the two companies. Inevitably, you'll start out talking the most—ideally about 75 percent. This percentage should shift to 50 percent during the meeting as you discuss your value and the other company's situation. Formatting your slides like this will help you create a back-and-forth discussion. For example, add these questions after the slides:

- **Problem slide**—"What challenges are you facing?"

- **Solutions**—"What solutions have you considered? How are other companies' products similar/different to ours?" (Please don't disclose any confidential information.)

- **Competition**—"What's your take on the market? Where do you see us fitting in?"

- **Custom slide(s)**—"What did you think of our value proposition and suggested synergies?"

- **Last slide**—"How would you like to continue?" or "What are the next steps?"

In follow-up meetings, the presentation should shift more to solving the company's specific needs and should focus on solutions. It's always a good sign if the lighthouse account is doing more talking than you—keep that in mind.

Three Keys to a Believable Story

All of that is great, but what *really* seals the deal? It's the most believable story that has three attributes: consistency, impact, honesty.

CONSISTENCY WINS

Consistency is one of Cialdini's seven principles of persuasion and something I hammered every time I met a customer. He says, "To understand why consistency is so powerful a motive, it is important to recognize that in most circumstances consistency is valued and adaptive."[8] Any story you tell about your company needs to express your company's steadiness and sturdiness. The most transformative deals will be the long-term ones, and no company wants to get in bed with a startup that delivers its product less than 99.99 percent of the time—especially in your service-level agreement (SLA). Over a long time, a low failure rate adds up. Steady as she goes!

Tell clients about the commitments you've fulfilled in the past. You can say, "In this deal, we promised our buyer we'd close this gap, and we did. Would you like to speak to them?" I remember telling one game client, "We told you two months ago we'd deliver on this product feature that you said you wanted, and we did. *Right on time*. Do you trust what I'm telling you?" He signed right after that and put us head-to-head against our competitor.

Furthermore, calling attention to your startup's consistent rate of evolution can be an effective tactic. "You can see how our product has evolved in 12 months—much more than any of our competitors'. Who do you want to work with as the best partner?" That's always a valuable line. Of course, you better have a good track record before pitching this advice.

IMPACT WINS

Established companies are busy and don't want to be bothered with petty deals. If you're going to get them to move, you must have a compelling story that will impact their bottom line, give them a growth wave, or provide global expansion. Dealing in Japan taught me the patience of working with slow-moving companies. But when you land a Japanese lighthouse, you had better believe they will put their might behind it. To do that, your technology needs to have core intellectual property or provide something your prospect can't do or execute within a reasonable time. It must fill a relatively large gap that they otherwise cannot do or that they don't find core to their strategy.

To demonstrate this point, here's what Mark Jacobstein (a serial entrepreneur with five exits) said in an interview: "To land large partnerships, you have to demonstrate that you'll impact someone's bottom line, for example, driving up to $100 million revenues. To do this, a startup must bring substantial IP, an active user base, or some other costly and time-consuming asset to build. Otherwise, these companies may brush you off as a feature they can build themselves." Mark ran a mobile voice over IP (VOIP) company called iSkoot (which later was acquired by Qualcomm) that worked with Skype and wireless companies like AT&T and Verizon. Although iSkoot's technology was useful for a period, Skype and AT&T owned the customer and had a direct relationship with each other. Both communication companies deemed this as core to their strategy and squeezed out iSkoot, developing the software themselves. So do something they can't or won't do.

HONESTY WINS

An intelligent customer will see right through any fast-talking and question your ability to close the gaps you identify. When it comes to sophisticated deals, be honest with the customer. Admit any shortcomings, missteps, or inconsistencies you might have in tandem with what you are doing to improve. Telling the truth is easier to remember as well. Being caught in a lie is not an easy thing to rectify.

I once heard a quote that went something like this: Tell the truth 99 percent of the time, so when you need to lie, they won't know. That strategy may work, but I have a better way to frame this: Pick and choose your words so that they are, indeed, correct statements and truthful. If you said that your product does X and it doesn't do it, that's a lie. But if you claimed your product does Y but didn't talk about X, then that's the truth. So tell the truth 100 percent of the time by being selective about what you say, and you'll save yourself and your post-deal team headaches.

What if your competitor falsifies something? Call your competitor out. If you think the client has been sold a lie, tell them so. Ask the customer, "Do you know if they are telling the truth? Maybe you should ask for proof." Do as much as you can to call into doubt their assertion.

Instead of twisting the truth, we won a handful of deals at Boku by being honest about our shortcomings while selling our strengths. When asked how we could outperform one of our competitors in their local market in Europe, I replied frankly, "We can't. At best, we will be on par with them, but we *will* outperform them in all of the markets combined, i.e., our total sum will be higher." The local market in Europe was only one slice of the pie. By being honest with our shortcomings, the company trusted us and bought into our strategy. That partnership was a big success all around.

Your Story versus Your Competitors'

Your relation to your competition will always throw some sort of a blemish in your otherwise perfect story. No one company has all the competitive advantages. It's a high-stakes game, and talk can get ugly, but don't take the low road.

If you completely dismiss the threat of your competitor, you'll be an obvious bullshitter. Bullshitting isn't a good look if you're trying to land a multimillion-dollar account. Talking about your competitors isn't going to be easy or comfortable, but there are a few tried-and-true ways to get past the discomfort and present your company in a favorable light. Your competitor may also speak poorly of you, so you need to nip it in the bud. Here are three ways to do this, which I've learned through some hard knocks: frame the conversation to your liking, downplay your competitors' advantages, and sell a brighter future. This advice is also the basis for more to come in Chapter 16.

FRAME THE CONVERSATION YOUR WAY

No matter how much you want to, don't disparage your competitors; it will make you look bad to polished buyers. There are ways to frame the discussion to make it look like you respect them, but you have distinct differences that make your solution more appealing. Be careful what information you leave behind, and don't let unvoiced doubts be the lingering variable that loses you the deal.

First, frame the conversation up front. I always liked to start conversations about competitors by saying something like this: "Company X is a good competitor; they drive us to be better, but we think our advantages are X, Y, and Z, and we can prove those with examples A, B, and C from real customers."

Second, reframe accusations. After many of your meetings, you will have a good idea of what scuttlebutt your competitor may be spreading about you. When this happens, face the challenge. Acknowledge their accusations. Say things like, "I'm aware that you may have heard the following things about us. Let me address those claims." If the allegations are particularly false, disproving a competitor's statements undermines credibility and can put you at an advantage. If they are true, you will get points for being up front and communicating openly. That's how you frame their accusations to your advantage.

By the way, don't leave behind any material or slides calling out a competitor. Your numbers could be wrong, and if the competitor ends up getting their hands on your data, you could get sued. For instance, a competitor once threatened to sue Boku because, on our competitive chart, we indicated a feature they didn't have, which they argued they did. It's best not to resort to attacks since they're rarely pleasant or conducive to good business. Delete any slides that may cast your competitors in a losing position.

Third, uncovering unvoiced doubts or concerns may be what makes or breaks a deal. I've lost deals because I never addressed an unvoiced competitor's accusation or concern about my company's product; the client just assumed that what they'd been told—by a competitor—was correct. How unbelievably frustrating! That lesson taught me always to find out what scuttlebutt the competition is spreading and address those points in meetings. It's better to do the talking and question-asking; never lose a deal because you didn't ask the question, "What do you think you already know about us?" or "What concerns do you have that I'm not addressing?" Uncover the unrevealed and then frame it to your advantage.

DOWNPLAY YOUR COMPETITORS' ADVANTAGES

There are several ways to downplay your competitors' advantages. The two points for this are to estimate the time to replicate the advantage and to quantify the advantage. As mentioned in the last chapter, advantages are only a function of time, so point out how easy it is to replicate the features. You can acknowledge that although, yes, your competitors do have some impressive and threatening advantages, they are not necessarily sustainable. What some companies think is a competitive advantage may only be a feature, a short-term stopgap, or even worse, something patched together to make them look pretty on slides (we call this vaporware or vapor slides). If your feature set is more sustainable and has a high cost to replicate, then let them know the engineering hours it would take to do so. Remember, time is a variable in competitive advantages.

Additionally, quantify your competitor's advantages. Differentiating yourself doesn't even require a perfect knowledge of the competing business. Ask your target customers to quantify and show you your competitor's advantage because, as you'll find out, customers often don't question the validity of each competitor's assertions. When you have the comparative numbers in front of you, you can likely point out that the discrepancies are not as disparate as they think. I'll discuss more about how to do this in Chapter 16.

SELL THE FUTURE, THEN DELIVER IT

Reframing the conversation toward the future can also help tell your story differently from your competitors. By focusing on your plans, you can give the buyer a feeling that you will make a better long-term partner by providing new technology and helping them enter new markets. There are two ways to do this.

In the section "Consistency Wins," I spoke about selling past performance. This time, sell the future. What gaps do you see ahead of your business, and how do you plan to fill them? What are your competitive advantages now, and what will they be down the road? As I mentioned before, there is nothing more impressive to a potential customer than telling them what you will do and then doing it. Go ahead and call your shot if you want to inspire trust and confidence in your company.

Next, reframe the competition and your competitive position. Your lighthouse account will lump you in with the also-rans, but your vision may be bigger than your competitors'. As an example, when Boku redefined the competitors as prepaid/gift card companies, we opened new doors. We became better partners for our existing customers and got the attention of the marketplaces like Sony and Apple. I vividly remember several customers saying, "We didn't think that you could compete with gift cards, but your solution is much more customer-friendly than theirs. If you provide a lower-cost solution compared to prepaid cards and a seamless technology into our platform, we are in." This remark focused us on what we needed to do to cross the chasm to a larger market. Think bigger because bigger competitors always make you better.

A RACE TO THE FUTURE: A BATTLE BETWEEN BOKU AND ZONG

Selling the future can be a race for startups. Take, for instance, this crazy anecdote in Boku versus Zong (our incumbent competitor). In the early days, we interviewed a recent MBA graduate/potential hire and discussed the idea of making a wallet product for mobile. This person went to our competitor, Zong, with that same idea. We mulled it over but decided the product would be of little use to our merchants (the companies who adopted our payments product for use by their customers). Strategically, Boku invested in global coverage rather than a new payment type.

Zong thought differently; they built the wallet product, sold it, and the market bought it, hook, line, and sinker.

Unbelievable! They asserted that it would save their merchants a lot of money—if and only if the merchants' consumers converted. Unfortunately for Zong, customers *didn't* convert, which is what we at Boku had expected. Suddenly, the merchants were looking to us for global coverage. We successfully made an acquisition to increase our global footprint. But was this enough to win?

Boku sold global access; Zong sold lower fees, as low as credit cards. Our story was, "If you want up to 100 markets, work with us. We'll be there in half a year." Their story was, "If you want lower fees—as low as credit cards—in a few markets, go with us." Their logic didn't make sense to us because we weren't competing with credit cards; we were serving customers without them. Staying focused over the next year, we beat them on a global execution strategy and were able to take most of their existing customers, including most of Facebook's traffic, by nearly three to one.

Did Zong win, or did we win?

Although we won the race with our customers, Zong won another race unexpectedly. Their vision appealed to PayPal, who was so convinced their new product was the future that they paid more than $150 million to acquire it, and the team retained high-level executive positions at PayPal and then Facebook (which I still find odd since they lost to Boku in the battle for the Facebook credits account). Post-acquisition, PayPal realized little value in the product and shut it down. Over time, Boku went on to fight a different battle and endured to an IPO and a company that flourishes as of this writing. Either way you look at it, the point is this: we both sold a story about the future and won, respectively.

CHAPTER 5

SHOVE OFF TO HIGH SEAS AND START HUSTLING

"No matter how many noes, maybes, or silent responses you get, you have to keep knocking. Never take things on face value; knock again, until you get a definitive response."

—Dan Steif, Chief Revenue Officer at Full Circle Fund,
ex-Boku, ex-Quip/Salesforce, ex-Google

Until now, your work has been heads down, strategizing, and planning where you'll go and what you'll say. It's time to push off into open seas and test the waters ahead. Your goal: find product interest which indicates the way to the lighthouse (or else wither at sea). To do that, you will have to form and test your hypotheses through your initial meetings—the dogs that bark. Taking that feedback, you can narrow your course to one or two potential paths.

Armed with your pipeline analysis and presentation, you shove off to the high seas—that is, chaos. Your job is to make some structure around it by gathering on-the-ground market information to determine product interest.

Before you set sail, prime your mind for success. Then hit the ground running. Define your hypotheses, be first to attain leads, win their interest, test your hypotheses, and don't let them ghost you.

Write Your Hypotheses

Before shoving off, you need to choose a direction based on the analysis you did. Sure, it's speculative, but you have to start somewhere. That's where the hypotheses come into play. Combining your lighthouse framework and strategic positioning, you could form a few hypotheses. The hypotheses are leading ideas that will help you find lighthouse customers who are interested in your product. Hypotheses may consist of most likely customers, which products will help you win the deal, and which existing customers will be adequate references for them. Such as:

- Deals X, Y, Z are likely to be the ones that need our product the most and one of them can be a lighthouse.

- If we close tier 2 deals A, B, C, then we are in better position to win a lighthouse.

- I need to have a product with the following features to win the lighthouse.

Whatever your hypotheses might be, keep them simple and clear. That's your guiding light as you shove off the port. Undoubtedly, with new information, these will change.

Ready Your Mind

Before setting out, just as you would prep the ship, prime your mind for success. Know what you're trying to achieve and how to respond to what may be thrown back at you. Without that, you're on a dead-end course to nowhere. Remember that your objective is to find product interest, not product fit—that comes in Chapter 15.

Here are a few tips to help with this process:

1. First, define a meeting schedule and the information that supports or refutes your lighthouse hypotheses. Know what information you want to uncover.

2. As I mentioned, most good sales/BD people can manage about 30 accounts, so set up 30 meetings. If a company doesn't meet your requirements, eliminate it and focus on the next deal.

3. Don't get too attached to or fixated on one account. Your goal is to tap the network and gain information. Don't assume you know who likes you or your product and who doesn't. Figure that out on your own by meeting with as many companies as you can.

4. By default, many people at corporations think they know more than you or have the upper hand—in fact, that may be the case. Be ready to deal with egos, pushbacks, and off-putting responses. Lose your ego and come back for more.

5. Know when to "touch and go" versus when to go deep in a conversation. When a deal isn't a fit, politely bow out or kindly let them know. Say, "Thank you for your time. I'll be in touch." Spend more time with people who seem to be as interested as you in discussing your pitch.

6. Identify time sucks. Work swiftly and with accurate information. Missteps like inaccurate market assessment or feedback, sluggish action, or an inability to reach a relevant or responsive contact in a timely fashion are not acceptable. One of the highest risks to your success is spending a lot of time on an immovable deal.

7. Don't let anyone ruffle your feathers—always be level-headed. You may feel like a pinball bouncing around with all the various responses, but just stay focused on what you are trying to achieve, remain committed to your plan, and leave your emotions elsewhere. Detach. Detach. Detach.

Be First to the Deal via Warm Introductions

With a ready mind, let's get going. Timing is everything. In Chapter 3, in the section "Use BD to Execute the Course," I said get to the lighthouse first. The vicissitudes of the sales cycles vary from client to client, but they all go through the same process. To control the conversation and timing as much as possible, it's better to be on the front end of the sales curve rather than playing catch-up.

Get ahead through warm leads. Call any relevant connection at other companies as soon as you can. The best way to generate leads at this stage is through investors, advisors, and your colleagues' networks. Warm introductions give you credibility, even if you are unproven. If your competitor gets a warm lead and you come in cold, you'll likely start at their heels. Making first contact also shows that you are a thought leader, gives you knowledge about the accounts your competitors are (or aren't) involved with, and most importantly, puts your cards in play. Warm leads are the best way to strike first.

So what happens when you've exhausted all the warm leads and, as can sometimes happen, still haven't reached two-thirds of your target list? Start hustling.

Start Hustling: Generate Cold Leads

As the Hustle Award winner for Davidson College Baseball Team, I know how to hustle leads better than anyone. If utilizing your network doesn't get the results you want, you will have to track leads down, most likely at conferences. There are four ways to procure contacts at an event.

First, the best way is to be a speaker. Speakers get an inbound audience and attention from the crowd. Dorie Clark, top-ranked business communications leader, told me in an interview at the Duke Executive Education Conference, "By being a speaker, make people come to you. You don't want to be chasing others. Always be front and center."

The next move is pit-jumping—to go to sessions where the speaker is a target contact. After the session is over, rush the speaker's desk, give him/her your cocktail pitch, and swap cards. MBA students call this pit-jumping. They'll either like your zealousness or think you're too aggressive. I once had a CEO tattletale to my CEO that I was too aggressive when trying to get an intro. Do it with a smile and "I look forward to hearing back from you."

The third is "event-working," which refers to wandering the floor, picking out name tags, and introducing yourself. It's like playing the lottery. Maybe, just maybe, you'll meet a match. Good event networkers must be a bit insane. They must be on their toes and catch people as they pass, either by looking at their badges or making random conversation. It can work if you like to play the lottery.

The last move I call nighttime networking, or "night-working." A few drinks at a crowded bar is often the best way to spend a little extra time getting to know people. Even better, let them talk, and they may disclose information about competitors or the market—after a few martinis. Nothing beats a nightcap when seeking information.

In 2019, I went to a financial technology (fintech) conference to put my old skills to the test, and I gathered data around it. Here's what I found. I was able to get responses from 18 out of 40 leads, with one tier 1 deal moving into late-stage discussions after three months.

The breakdown was as follows:

Event working	8 responses/17 contacts
Pit-jumping	2 responses/5 contacts
Visiting booths	2 responses/8 contacts
Night-working	6 responses/10 contacts + some valuable follow-up information

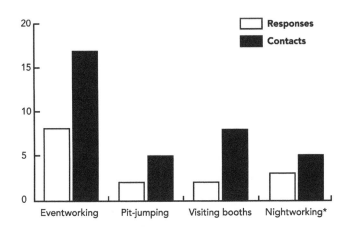

Cold Leads at Events

What the results reveal is that ships passing in the night don't get quality leads. The more quality time I spent with my targets, the more likely they were to return my follow-up. I defined quality time as being able to walk through my value proposition slowly and get their feedback. Night-working was more effective than event-working. Visiting booths and pit-jumping were touch and go. Although I received many business cards, visiting booths was rarely beneficial because the person I wanted to meet was usually very busy with preset meetings, and most likely the booth workers' goal was to sell, not to be sold to. So I swiftly swapped cards and met them later in the conference. For the meetings in which I spent more than a minute or two, my response rate significantly increased—that's a quality lead.

Dan Steif also gives a testament to this strategy. "When I was at Google, I could call anyone, and they'd pick up," he says. "But when I joined Boku, no one knew who we were and often wouldn't return emails or introductions. To expand into a new vertical of magazines, I tried pit-jumping, following Kurt's event strategy tactics: show up during the last five minutes of a session, give the cocktail pitch, quickly swap cards with the person you want to meet, ask to meet them later at the event, and jump to the next breakout session. I'd have another meeting with them at the conference, then weeks later, I had a dozen meetings, and months later, I closed our first deals."

In a time when no conferences are held, such as a pandemic, we have to adjust. Now the Chief Revenue Officer at Full Circle Fund, Dan contributes with the following tips on generating leads in a pandemic.

GENERATING LEADS IN A PANDEMIC

With the COVID-19 pandemic came a new question: how do we generate leads during a shutdown? Dan and I sat down and worked on a process to answer this question. Digital sales tools are on the rise and, even more, will surface in the coming years. This section isn't a synopsis of them all; instead, it focuses on a process to help you generate leads. Plug and play any tool you deem appropriate.

Step 1: Fill the lead pipeline

Filling the pipeline isn't as easy as it sounds. To do so efficiently, you need a solid matching score for the right companies and verticals, as discussed in Chapter 2. Ideally, you will have three or four verticals of 100+ companies—and that's just the beginning. Now pick your favorite customer relationship management (CRM) tool. Fill 'em up, assign team members, and off you go.

Step 2: Identify deal leads

This part is the most challenging part in a pandemic. You still have your investors' and colleagues' networks, but when those are all tapped out, what's next? It's time to pound the internet pavement. The best online tools for list building and lead creation are LinkedIn Sales Navigator, ZoomInfo, UpLead, and Seamless. The filters in LinkedIn Navigator allow you to sort by seniority, function, and years of experience. You can click and export that list to Seamless, where you can easily access anyone's email and phone number. Then send that contact data back into your CRM directly or via a CSV (comma-separated values) file.

Step 3: Automate your outreach

It's best to have a multifaceted outreach to increase the probability of a response. One way to do this is to automate your outreach using Groove, Outreach, and HubSpot. To start this process, create a flow that includes phone calls, emails, and LI connection request + messages. The more automated, the better, *but you must personalize your initial outbound emails*. Say something about your contact's latest update, the university they attended, or a shared connection.

Dan stresses that the cadence of communication is the way you hook leads. Making an initial request through all channels should be done in a single week to allow you to sift through responses and prioritize the ones who are interested. Otherwise, you may wait too long to hook them. You don't know who already wants your product, so don't spray the pipeline over months; do it all at once. Once connected, follow up with your contact weekly with check-in items, including updates from your company and questions about where they are in their selection process. (More on this in Part 3.) Keep a steady cadence and ask to meet with them biweekly. Dan says, "Get on their schedule as quickly as possible. Be presumptuous. Send them a calendar invite, especially if they agree to continue the discussions. Then you are in the driver's seat to push it along. Make them tell you they aren't ready for it yet." Get them to buy into your cadence and the cycle will flow smoothly.

Step 4: Track your sales operations

Next, measure your progress. Measurement, optimization, and coaching tools like ClearSlide, Mindtickle, Chorus.io, Gong.io, Scratchpad, Trywingman.com, and Execvision.io can track what people click on and what people say, and they can analyze how to optimize your sales funnel. It's helpful to find out what touch points are working for you and determine the most effective way to communicate with your clients.

Note that even after it is long past, the pandemic will have forever changed the culture of sales and BD. Receivers are now far less likely to ignore inbound emails. Opportunities that once came from face-to-face conversations now pop up in your inbox. Sales tools, alternatives to LinkedIn, and automated outreach tools have become more pervasive and accepted. Overall, with less travel and fewer conferences, I sincerely believe that doing business will become more efficient and less stressful for the outbound salesperson.

This is a good time to give a plug to a community I've been involved with for a few years called Modern Sales Pros (MSP). Should you have any questions about salaries/commissions, tools, or even leads that are hard to get ahold of, just query the community and voilà! MSP is the world's largest community for revenue leaders in the sales space, including management, operations, enablement, strategy, and development. Their mission is to create an environment for members to get answers to questions they'd struggle to solve on their own. Further, they partner with thought leaders and world-class organizations to build educational programs that inform, challenge, and create connections among members so they can achieve their highest potential.

Win Their Interest

When you first meet a prospective customer, you must win their interest in both you and the product. Sounds easy, right? Wrong. The almost foolproof method to do this is to make the right first impression, get information from them, and then follow up tactically. Whatever you do, don't hard sell up front.

So, then, how should you make a good first impression? I have four basic rules:

1. Walk like a giraffe. Have a good posture and show confidence. Keep your head above the crowd as if you are someone they should be speaking to.

2. Speak incisively. That means speak crisply, quickly, and clearly. Think about slicing a piece of fruit. That's how you should speak.

3. Be unassuming and approachable. It helps to always have a smile on your face and open arms. Standing cross-armed with a frown won't open any doors.

4. Show interest. Just being genuinely interested in the other person and their business goes a long way.

Drop the ego. As mentioned earlier, you will learn to deal with a lot of big egos at these companies. To alter that, you must be deferential. Boost their egos! Make sure you don't fight ego with arrogance or overconfidence. The best way to be is unassuming and unpretentious. *So ditch the ego.* If they boast, agree; tell them they are great but could be greater if they had a minute or two to listen to you. You want them to think, "I'd like to work with this person; they seem easy to get along with and can add value."

It ain't a dog-and-pony show about your company! Don't forget that the reason you're here is to gain information. Throughout the course of your conversation, think about your spreadsheet. What are your dependent variables? Are your assumptions correct? Is there product interest? By asking your contact questions, you'll not only get answers, but you'll also create a 50-50 conversation that will make following up more straightforward later. Here are a few lines to get them to exchange information in the dialogue:

- "Would you be interested in personal introductions so we can get to know each other a bit?" *Too many people just jump right into the business talk.*

- "Before I get started, what do you know about us?" *It may surprise you what competitors will tell prospective companies in hopes of landing a deal.*

- "I appreciate your interest in us. Before we begin, please tell me about your company and how we can help you."

Agree on how to follow up. End your first conversation by asking if you can follow up by email with links or collateral. Even better, get them to agree to the next meeting in person or on Zoom. If they agree, then they are on the hook, and you have the right to hold them accountable. Don't be afraid to start your email with "You agreed that..." or "You aren't being a responsive partner..."

Be tactical. Finally, when you follow up after the first discussion, do so with precision. In an interview with Mark Gerban, an American business executive in Europe, he advised against sending a generic deck to larger companies—you risk it getting tossed aside. In advance, ask for a phone call or meeting to go over your value proposition. He continues:

> Don't spitball random ideas about how you could work together. Larger companies may not know what you do, and you only have their attention for a short time. Your short deck should encompass several meetings in one: a brief overview, a mock-up or flowchart explaining how you could work together, with a few options (custom slides), and an idea about the business model (without actual prices).

This slide deck is the standard sales deck I explained in Chapter 4. And keep it short in case it falls into a competitor's hand. By the way, a good rule of thumb is not to attach any documents to your email but to ask for that second meeting instead. It's always better to get them on the phone to go over it together. It leaves less subject to interpretation.

LEAD SOFT; DON'T HARD SELL

Early in the conversation, *don't hard sell*. As Mark mentioned, explain how you could work together, with a few options. Get to know them, and wait until you know what they want. That means you can't pitch just one aspect of your selling points or competitive advantages. You pitch the wrong point, and the door is closed. Stay high level with your discussions, and ask questions until you zero in on their needs. Ask questions, ask questions, ask questions. When they tell you what they are looking for, then you tailor your sales points to them. I'll discuss this more in Chapter 14.

Don't Let Ghosting Spook You

People respond lots of different ways, especially when they are confused. Few say no. Many say, "Maybe, let's keep talking." Others say, "I'm interested" but then don't respond so long that the anxiety builds in the top of your head. Whether it's dating or the business world, you will get ghosted. Here is your proton pack to be a ghostbuster.

What should you do if your contacts ghost you? What if you don't hear back? Whatever you do, don't harass them. That will only lessen your chance of success. Instead, let it go. If that contact doesn't respect you enough to respond after a few emails, they're probably not worth talking to anyway. (In Japan, this would never happen. It's dishonorable not to respond to someone with whom you've previously spoken.) Don't take it personally; remember it's part of the game.

Remember that big companies are busy, and it may take a while to engage them. Dorie Clark recommends not bombarding someone, following up with them weekly for only a few weeks, and being respectful. You can also try texting or Facebook messages. "Hi, I haven't heard back. I know you are busy, but if you're still interested, please let me

know. If now's not a good time, I can always follow up in a few months!"
Here are a few I like:

- "Sorry to be a pest, but I'm just following up on these items."

- "When we met, we agreed on these next steps. I'm working diligently on my side, so when will you be able to return this information?"

- "Has the circumstance changed since we last spoke? Please let me know."

- "How was your fall/winter/summer vacation? Would be great to hear where you went and get an update..." *Talking about vacations is an unassuming way to get the conversation going again.*

If those don't work, stalk them, I guess. The CEO of one of our competitors at Boku was a Facebook-utilizing machine. He friended every potential partner, engaged them with his family, and invited them to social events. He made them feel so very special and became their temporary friend for the deal. One target even told me, "He friended me on Facebook, and now we chat all of the time about our kids. He's such an amazing guy." His tactic made me want to vomit, but it worked. By the way, talking about your kids is a great get-to-know tactic. Although I thought it was intrusive, he stalked almost everyone, and it worked for him.

Always be networking, especially within companies in the land of those trillion-dollar transformational deals. They have complex organizational charts with moving pieces. It's critical to build relationships with a network of people in the same company early in the game. One of your objectives is to find the right person who can lead a deal and become your deal champion (you'll hear this term often from here on). This is important because your initial contact might not be the right person to lead your deal. If three or four contacts point you to the same person at their company, you know you've got the right one. If you are getting mixed signals, though, keep networking; other contacts could come in handy as a "friendly" when you need to backchannel for information. (More about this in Chapter 14.)

Last, don't take it personally if they ghost you or even if you get slimed; keep going back at it until they turn into Gozer the Destructor (the villain in *Ghostbusters*).

A Tale of Four Leads

Boku's four most significant leads came through different channels. We progressed through each timeline with varying levels of efficiency and speed. Luckily, as the below examples illustrate, leads will happen for you, too, if you're relentless enough.

Sony—This lead is an example of "swarming the org," which I discuss in depth in Chapter 9. To win this deal, we enrolled almost the entire hierarchy of Sony. I initially met Sony's head of payments by visiting their booth at an E3 conference. I followed up as usual but couldn't create any concrete plans. Then one of our investors, Andreessen Horowitz, hosted Sony executives at their office and introduced them to their portfolio companies, including us. It was there that we met Joseph Tou in Corporate Development who became our internal support, setting up meetings for us in Europe and pushing the business units to work with us (more about this in Chapter 14). Through his support, we quickly forged a relationship with the Sony PlayStation team in the United States, who then routed us to meetings in Europe. By connecting with the Sony team globally at the Mobile World Congress (MWC), we finally found our deal champion, who was based out of Europe. It took a total team effort from our US and Europe offices to convince Sony that we were the right partner. From there, it took one year to hammer out a deal. That's an example of how you swarm the org.

Microsoft—Persistence, to a fault. Our Founder, Ron, initially met Microsoft after speaking on a panel. To start the deal, we pushed the Microsoft payments team internally. Thanks to an investor introduction, we set up meetings with Xbox to discuss Boku's value-add for console games. Additionally, we utilized our partnership with Nokia—which Microsoft had recently acquired—to influence the payments team's decision. Along this line, we continued doing custom products for Nokia at a loss to increase the probability that Microsoft would work with us. (I'll address doing custom work in Part 3.) Because of re-org after re-org and new lead after new lead, it took nearly five years from the first meeting to finally close the deal.

Google—Old colleagues make the most fruitful leads. In 2012, Boku hired Dan Steif, a former salesman for Google, who had friends in Google's corporate development team. Dan's friends helped us get in touch with the right people, and although we never landed a direct deal with Google, we still became an approved vendor for their in-house payments platform. That was a win for our BD team, and it shows that success can come in a variety of forms. Hiring people from companies you want to do a deal with is an aggressive move, one that may be warranted when that company could be a transformational deal, bringing in the big bucks. We all know that friends do deals with friends.

Apple—Some leads just come down to luck. People often rotate jobs within an industry, so even if a new contact doesn't provide any immediate leads, it's always good to make random friends. During our years running around conferences, Ron had spoken on a panel with an investment banker who later joined Apple. Once his friend joined, Ron reconnected, and he and I discussed potential partnership opportunities between the two companies. This relationship eventually led to Boku's deal with Apple. It was precisely the type of partnership we wanted and almost too good to be true. On the back of Sony's success, our deal with Apple closed in only 18 months. That wasn't luck.

Part 1 Review

What I discussed in Part 1 is the basics of BD. Nail them and you will be confident in the chart you mapped out. Let me repeat: nail them and you will be confident in the direction you choose. That unflappable confidence will keep you on course through the high tides and choppy seas. You'll hire a BD Captain who is perseverant and loyal to your company. Your analysis will help you logically bifurcate your GTM strategy between BD and sales deals and pick your lighthouse accounts. Create a strategy that will put your product and market presence in the clear lead, and use BD as a strategic tool to chart your course. If you have to, draw it all out on a map; the map or pitch deck is your story. Prepare your pitch deck well before you head out into open seas. Once you do, gather market surveillance so that you can get your team excited to join you on your journey ahead in Part 2.

GALVANIZE YOUR CREW AND MANEUVER THE SHIP FOR STORMY SEAS

"The meat and potatoes for your team!"

CHAPTER 6

CREATE DEAL PLANS TO PREPARE YOUR TEAM

"Success depends upon previous preparation, and without such preparation, there is sure to be a failure."

–Confucius[9]

The first part of this book has prepared you—maybe even overprepared you—to chart an optimized course to lighthouse accounts. You've even dipped your toes in the waters. With new market information from your barking dogs, you've updated your lighthouse framework, and a few leads shine bright. You have a reasonable strategy and a strategy with no priorities is just a wish list. So take that information and create your deal plan, prioritize your actions, and guide yourself and your team for the long voyage ahead.

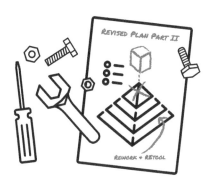

Each lighthouse gets a plan, or you'll sail your ship in the dark. I'm always amazed by the number of companies who expect an unfortunate salesperson to close a million-dollar deal with no direction aside from "good luck." In this case, rarely does luck work, so let's just be dadgum good. To be good, you need to be thoughtful. Just as product managers plan using scrums, Gantt charts, and the like, your BD team should analyze every account from every possible angle, including sales angles, strategies, and time schedules. That way, even in the dark, you'll know what you are doing.

So, then, how do you make a deal plan? A deal plan is a structured plan that consists of a hypothesis, a written document with action items, a list of contacts, milestones, and more. Not just for you, this plan is for your team to get them organized and show them the ropes. Do this with detail and dedication, and the deals are yours to win.

Step 1: Update Your Hypotheses

Update your hypotheses with a more granular plan. Your initial conversations should have given you enough information to create a plan with a more detailed recipe. For instance:

To win the deal [X], I hypothesize that

- I need to be the market leader in industry [Z] with the widest geographic reach;

- I need to have product with the highest conversion rate; and

- I need a technology that can scale quickly to service hundreds of millions of users, particularly in Asia.

Whatever your hypothesis might be, keep it simple and clear. That's your guiding light.

Step 2: Create a Deal Plan

We all know the business proverb "What gets measured, gets managed." Even though BD successes are by nature immeasurable, the deal plan can help you quantify your progress and improve morale and motivation. It can also be a good measuring stick for your executive team to track progress—that is, what's working and what isn't.

Before you write anything, consider your audience. Your audience is anyone at any level involved with the deal. The basis for action and progress, the plan helps you track the deal and follow what's happening. Most audience members will be part of the deal team. Others might be investors or advisors who can make introductions and help push the deal forward when needed. Either way, it gets and keeps everyone up to speed. Keep them all in mind when you write it.

Make it shareable. Whether this can be done on Salesforce, Scratchpad, Upland (Altify), Pipedrive Trackable Sales Documents, or just Google Docs, the scale of the operation may be as large as 20–30 people. Whatever you choose, make it easily accessible to everyone. These days, it's common for product managers, lawyers, and engineers to log in to Salesforce or Pipedrive. Even easier, you can use a secure Google document, which can be easily accessed, updated, and sent to many parties, even those not full time.

COMPONENTS OF THE DEAL PLAN

1) Hypotheses

State it here.

2) The Overview

This is a quick rehashing of the market context, background, and any salient points to have up front.

3) Action Items

The action item section will undergo the most change of any part of the deal plan. You'll keep a record of the next set of steps the BD team needs to take in the deal-making process. If kept up to date, the action item list minimizes the potential for redundant moves and confusion over who should be doing what. To keep it simple, cap its length at five items at any one time. I'll discuss the spreadsheet you'll need for other, smaller action items in the next section.

4) Selling Points

This section is a quick summary of your key selling points, deal structure, and pricing. It's crucial to track this with other team members like legal, finance, and the CEO.

5) Product Requests

Underneath the action items, you should list out the key requests you'll need for deal closure. These aren't requests you make of your team but requests the lighthouse account makes of your business.

6) Roadblocks and Challenges

These are key sticking points for the deal to happen. Someone may have told you about them, or they might just be risks that you feel.

7) Next Steps

What are the next meetings, product development, finance, or legal next steps.

8) Main Contacts and Tier Up the Team

This section lists the main "ins" you have at an organization, their contact info, and whom you've assigned to be the point people for those contacts. This list may expand to a complete list of connections at the large account, which you'll need to develop a relationship with to complete the deal. Due to the length of time it can take to get in touch with some executives, you should assign a team member to each contact to foster the relationship. I'll discuss more about this in Chapter 9. Don't stop there: the more contacts the better.

9) Milestones

This section lists the goals you set up for you and your team. If you can set up a realistic timeline for your deal plan, you'll know for the next six months whether you're ahead or behind. Don't be afraid to make the goals for each month ambitious—as long as you don't confuse "ambitious" with "ludicrous."

EXAMPLE OF THE DEAL PLAN

Deal Team

- Kurt (BD), Jessica (Product), Jonathan (Marketing), Brian (Legal), David (CEO), Vinod (Board Investor), James (London)

Hypothesis: To win this deal, we need to show market leadership (top one or two) in industry [X], have a product with [Y] feature, and have international presence in [Asia].

Project Lighthouse Deal Overview:

- Lighthouse actively looking for solutions to solve problem [Y].
- Revenue potential is based on revenues from other vendors or what they've indicated. (Note: Always try to get potential deal size early.)
- Competitors in the deal include [A, B, C]. They've already discussed ideas with other companies. We are late to the game, so we must work fast.

Selling Points:

- **Timing**—We need to convince them that doing this NOW is better than WAITING. They lose money as they scale without our technology integrated.
- **Market forces**—Without this, they are at a competitive disadvantage.
- **Scalability**—We should give them the best long-term solution in terms of high-volume scalability, lowest price as scale, and transparent fees. Their volumes could be in transactions of millions.

- **Service**—We provide dedicated support professionals and 24/7 escalation support.
- **International angle**—Europe doesn't seem to be a priority, but Asia does.

Product Requests:

- One-tap checkout needed
- 30-day payment terms
- 24/7 support

Roadblocks/Challenges:

- Economics may not work out unless pricing can drop significantly with scale.
- Market-specific regulation of our service in Japan is highly regulated.
- Our partner's deal lead, Mike, has a close friend at a competitor—need to find a way to trump this relationship.

Key Next Steps:

- Get second meeting with deal partner; Mike has stated he gets our value but no indication on his preference. Can our CEO meet their CEO to influence his decision?
- Get sandbox development started to show our technical ease of integration.
- Develop custom pitch for product fit from marketing.
- Tier up contacts:
    7 Get board-level support fast to cut off the competition.
    7 Get CEOs to meet.
    7 Get engineers talking quickly and testing the product.

Contact List:

Partner Name	Location	Role	Our Team	Deal Role
Mike	SF	Director of Fulfillment	KD	VP of BD; Lead
Jack	SF	CEO	David	CEO; Executive Support
Vivek	NYC	Product Management	Jessica	VP of Product; find a product solution and product fit
Joseph	SF	Board Investor	Vinod	Investor; Board oversight
Jeremy	London	Head of European Product	James	GM of Europe, European expansion; make sure we scale in the EFIGS (England, France, Italy, Germany, Spain)
Dave	SF	CFO	Jon	CFO, pricing and payment terms
Wei	SF	Engineer	Angus	Engineer; technical specifications and integration
Jane	SF	Legal	Brian	Head of Legal; legal contract
Bella	SF	Partnership integration manager	Joanne	VP of Customer Success

Timeline	Milestones	Responsible
June	Get second meeting with Mike; get a meeting with the product team to discuss fit. Try to push quickly to sandbox environment.	Kurt/Jessica
July	Get Vinod to meet Joseph (board members) and let him know deal is going down.	David/Vinod
July	Get Angus to check in with Wei to check off on shared product specs.	Kurt/Angus
August	Get Mike/Jane to discuss high-level contract with lawyers to suss out any major roadblocks.	Kurt/Brian
September	Start a sandbox to test product with Angus and introduce Customer Success VP Joanne.	Kurt/Joanne
October	Get deal terms sorted and closed.	Kurt/Brian

Step 3: Prepare Your Deal Team

It's tough to close a deal as a one-person captain. Why? Frankly, the target company contact may get tired of hearing from you all the time. Moreover, the VP of BD can't know everything. Most large partnerships result from two sizable internal teams working together. If you are the sole BD person showing up in a room with a handful of product managers and engineers, you'll get glares full of doubts and question marks.

You don't need 10 teammates every time; just start with a handful. Think of a deal team like the five fingers on your hand. There are two sales members (one senior and one junior), a product expert, a lawyer, a technical integration manager, and a customer success or account manager—who will join toward the end. Without one of those fingers, you're going to do a lot of fumbling around.

That's the core team, but it may even extend beyond that. Max Lehmann, my old colleague from Boku who is now SVP of Business Development at Adyen (a global payments company), remembers closing a $2 billion deal with a rental car company in Europe. "To close the deal, the customer asked for the board of directors to meet to verify the capital structure and stability of the company. Big deals require boards to meet boards."

Because of the importance of working together as a team, your deal plan should also lay out the expectations and functions for each group involved. You'll find a general list of responsibilities below to build from:

- **Finance**—Sets pricing and payment terms.

- **Marketing**—Provides market analysis, presentation materials/ custom slides, and post-deal promotions.

- **Product**—Integrates documents, customized features, product limitations, and boundaries for pricing with finance.

- **Legal**—Notes what terms to avoid or be wary of, helps with formal communication, and notes what to say (and what not to say) when negotiating.

- **Executive**—Rallies the support by providing an executive-level overview, getting investors and advisors involved, and holding everyone accountable. Provides a key escalation path if the deal feels like it's going off the tracks.

Note that you may get pushback from your team about the deal plan. "That's not my job!" they may respond gruffly. To avoid this, the CEO should incentivize everyone working on the deal, whether through equity, shared commission, or a quarterly cash bonus. A shared upside sets the table for everyone to get involved and ensures that everyone participates in the victory. Alignment of rewards is a must.

Alignment of responsibility and communication is why a deal plan is essential. The deal plan clarifies the paths and timing of communication. It should be easily referenced and edited. It can work wonders to prevent miscues and failures. This foundation of team involvement also serves as the basis for a future request for proposal (RFP), which I cover in Chapter 9. Knowledge sharing and teamwork provide the team the alignment required to execute the plan.

Step 4: Continually Adjust the Plan

"Plans are useless, but planning is indispensable."

–Dwight D. Eisenhower[10]

Getting a bomb dropped on you—losing a big deal—is the best way to learn how to win deals. There are many reasons sales are lost. Some are lost because the product wasn't up to snuff. Other times, pricing was wrong. It could be that you didn't articulate your competitive advantages and differentiators distinctly enough. What's inexcusable, however, is letting deals fall through the cracks. It's *your fault* when you don't move quickly enough, don't respond adequately, or weren't prepared. It's frustrating when the customer goes silent or decides on another competitor without telling you, or chooses not to work with you. But it's *also your fault* if you didn't wedge yourself in the decision-making process to find out what was going on. At the very least, you should attempt to discover why they chose someone else and what you can do to improve—saving you your dignity but not your ship.

In the early days at Boku, we got an entire barrage of cannonballs. The blow that almost sank the ship came when we lost Facebook to our competitor, Zong. Zong was a first mover in the market and well ahead of us in terms of product, but we were catching up quickly, and they knew it. A Swiss company, Zong made an early decision to place their US office right in Palo Alto, right next to Facebook. Although we had a few early discussions with Facebook, they went completely silent on us until suddenly announcing a deal with Zong. Some say timing is everything; location is even more important, perhaps. (As an aside, the Buddha says there is no time, just place.) We were shocked.

Unwilling to give up, we reloaded to win Facebook back. We tasked three people to sell to different departments: payments, engineering, and BD departments. One of my engineering friends at the time by chance moved into Facebook's payments department and gave us the inside scoop. In addition, we climbed the executive ranks and involved our board members. All of this was outlined in a detailed plan, which was a monumental task.

The planning motivated the team and got them on the same page. Team members across multiple levels of the company worked on the new product idea, others in Europe and Asia built out new footprints, and the engineering team worked relentlessly to catch up, building a very custom product, which we then used to gain more clients. The team started working in sync.

The plan didn't evolve how we drew it out, however. We restocked our ship and acquired a competitor, Paymo, who added a broader coverage of countries. After six months of integration, we had a competitive advantage: we were available in 80 countries, while our competitor was available in only around 50. This meant more money for our merchants. The moment our product went live, we ran the table with online gaming merchants and quickly took and outperformed accounts who had been using Zong. These new Boku customers told Facebook and helped us get our foot back in the door. Losing pushed us to get better fast.

To complete the process, though, we needed even more ammo. Facebook wanted a specific billing application programming interface (API) that mirrored one of the credit cards. Their current provider didn't have

the incentive to invest in a proposition like this—they were already high
on the hog. That was our silver bullet. We were a more aggressive, committed partner who could provide them with broader coverage and a
new product fit. We had the desire; they didn't. In the end, we tweaked
the plan as we went along, but the plan is what got everyone focused on
the lighthouse deal.

CHAPTER 7

INTERNATIONAL PLANNING– RISK AND RETURN

"Through a modest investment, you can develop an understanding of a new market, then decide to go alone or partner."

—Thomas Clayton, global business executive and CRO at Bill.com

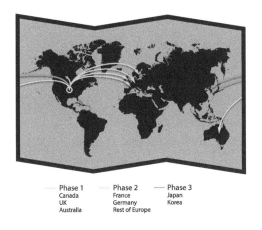

Phase 1	Phase 2	Phase 3
Canada	France	Japan
UK	Germany	Korea
Australia	Rest of Europe	

Common phased rollout plan for international expansion.

Your deal plans indicate one major gap: your lighthouse needs an international presence to support them. Initially, looking overseas (literally), you see many opportunities. Out of the corner of your eye, you see competition encroaching, causing you to change your mind; heading that way could be a distraction and take you off course. Stay focused and tap out your home market first, right? But what if the grass *is* greener on the other side? Truth be told, it's better not to just stay at home. If you want to play big, you'll need to go global and learn how to outmaneuver homegrown competitors.

Internally at Boku, we used to say our company was the smallest mobile global company in the world. It may have been. Although we employed only a few hundred people, we had offices in the United States, United Kingdom, Germany, Japan, India, Singapore, Brazil, and Greater China (Taiwan, Hong Kong, and mainland) because our customers needed us there. As we built out our international presence, we weren't sure which geographies would work, so we tested several out before investing significantly in any one market. Some markets didn't work, some took time, and others profited nicely. But by investing in those markets, even just a bit, we gained a suitable footprint and global product to win the lighthouse.

What's the best way to do this? Here's a cheat sheet. Before going abroad, be clear on the why, then prepare and analyze the markets. Do proper due diligence beforehand to know the lay of the land before placing bets. Find a partner with strategic, financial, and cultural alignment. Start small and then double down.

Why Invest Internationally?

Even the wealthiest tech companies with the most advanced sales teams have mixed results from international expansion. Google and Facebook, the two tech companies most primed for world domination, have failed in China. Companies like Twitter, Salesforce, and Boku have done spectacularly well in Japan. Still, on the whole, Japan has a bad rap for being slow to adopt technology and grow the market; this is finally changing. Japan does move slow, but when corporates partner, they commit to their partner and make it work. You might think gaining a footprint in Europe would be easy, but in Europe, clones of your business who are more familiar with local market regulations quickly copy you before you get the chance to expand there.

So if international expansion is so complex, why do it? Because if you want to win a lighthouse, you need to be global. Your first step toward this is to consider your why.

HAVE CLEAR OBJECTIVES FOR THE WHY

Begin by having a clear objective. A concrete goal will carry you and your startup through the ups and downs of expansion. There are five different reasons you may choose to go global:

Develop New Markets

You are riding a unicorn and your investors say, "Go global ASAP." In this case, you need to reduce your dependence on the markets you've developed in the United States. If your startup's product is niche enough, you can reach the domestic market's end quickly.

Block Clones

Along those lines, the global venture capital world moves fast. In a matter of months after announcing a new company, clones will pop up all over the world. Acquire and expand so that you stretch the seams without bursting them.

Serve Existing Customers

Serving existing customers is the most risk averse way to go global. For example, Sony PlayStation's headquarters in San Diego asked us to integrate the Japanese carriers, which gave us a compelling reason to set up in Japan and work directly with the big three carriers: Softbank, DoCoMo, and KDDI. Before Sony came along, those carriers saw us as a foreign company with no value to the local market, and they were right. The reason Sony asked us to do it was because their global billing was based in San Diego, and they had hired us to make their carrier payments globally.

Acquire Multiple Interested Customers

Sometimes startups win a customer by chance in a remote country. I've seen startups strike gold in unexpected lands—one winning a big customer in Indonesia and another in Australia. Both companies did an about-face and focused there; both deals sucked them dry and distracted them from the US market over time. Both failed. Only do that if they will be a very profitable customer in the long term. It's usually best to wait for interest from multiple customers in other markets before considering significant expansion.

Most Relevant: Land the Lighthouse

By showing global capabilities and presence, a startup is more likely to close the large deals it wants, rather than the deals that want them. These days, most foreign corporations have a Silicon Valley presence; start there, or start at the corporate headquarters (wherever that may be). They will point you to the markets that are important for them and ease your entry. When we worked with Facebook, they directed us to certain markets they required. Even in Japan where the local country manager wanted to cut us out, the Facebook headquarters mandated our relationship. For this reason, get a deal champion at your customer's headquarters to ensure victory.

Before You Go Abroad: Analyze and Prioritize

Prioritize international expansion opportunities the same way you did deal opportunities. The stakes of global expansion are much higher, so your analysis needs to be even more detailed than your lighthouse tables. Like with the lighthouse analysis, weigh your variables and create an equation to rank markets.

VARIABLES FOR ANALYSIS

With the help of global business executive Thomas Clayton, current CRO at Bill.com and the former VP of Global Operations at Houzz, I'll break down the five variables a startup should consider when going international and determining which markets they should target.

Macroeconomic/Market Size

What's the market size, and is it big enough to justify an investment? These variables will look like country GDP per capita, age demographics, internet users, and the specific market size for your industry.

Microeconomic/Market Assessment

Assess the demand for your product. These variables may seem abstract, but try to quantify them: the likelihood of switching, barriers to entry, rate of adoption, and price competition.

Competitive Landscape

Keenly assess your ability to compete locally. How many competitors exist? How formidable are they? What would be the cost for a customer to switch to you? In many local markets like Germany and Japan, customers are loyal and prefer to use local solutions. Max Lehmann says about Germany, "There is much national pride where local companies sell—we call them the local heroes. They have a stronghold on particular markets; it's tough to unseat them." Japan, too, has a homegrown financial services market that any foreign competitor has had trouble supplanting.

Regulation

Know the regulatory environment before going in headfirst. Some countries aggressively court foreign businesses; other countries uphold protective environments like China. Be sure to spend ample time researching the snags you might encounter while doing business. Regulations, withholding taxes, free trade agreements, political stability, business ethics, foreign IP protection, hiring/firing protections, and so forth can affect profits or you.

American technology business executive living in Europe Mark Gerban offers this example of financial services regulations:

> Outside of the UK, Europe tends to be more conservative than the US on several fronts. For instance, EU regulatory laws such as General Data Protection Regulation (GDPR) prevent the use of collection and use of personal data without the consumer's explicit consent. This consent affects many user flows and business models since data collection is essential for most software companies.

Geopolitics

The world changes. It's better to invest in places where the wind doesn't change directions overnight due to political unrest, currency inflation, or revolutions. Let your venture investors take the high-risk bets. Your priority should be to invest in developed countries with relatively lower political risk, then take on more risk gradually. Your seas are rough enough; don't choose to sail into even choppier waters.

Fundamental Conjectures

Your analysis will lead to even more questions. Which countries do you approach first? Which ones should you trade off? What will it take you to break even? What is your chance of success? At last, can you be a top-three player in the market?

When answering these questions, Thomas Clayton, who worked globally for two decades, advocates for clustering countries with similar markets and barriers to entry. A/B testing is also a way of trying out markets before significantly investing. Clayton says, "Group countries based on similarities along commercial, economic, political, and cultural dimensions. Often, these countries can be covered by the same country manager. In more complex markets like Asia, choose one country at a time because they can be time consuming."

In other words, slow and steady. You don't need world domination all at once. Just make sure to target the least challenging markets first. Here are a few:

1. The United Kingdom, Australia, and Canada are the natural first countries to expand from the United States. The United Kingdom had the advantage of being a launchpad for Europe, though Brexit may affect this launchpad status.

2. The first foreign-language countries are often Germany and France. They each have a well-developed market, a high GDP per capita, and a vibrant technology scene. For those two markets, separate country managers are needed, but the country manager for France can often cover Italy and Spain.

3. The Scandinavian countries can be lumped together: Sweden, Denmark, Norway, and Finland. These are very low-risk countries with high consumer purchasing power. In the last decade, they've stimulated startups within their countries, like Spotify, Rovio, King, and iZettle, so local competition has increased.

4. Start in Asia with Japan or Korea, close comparisons, so pick one or the other. Japan is a more considerable market opportunity and a bit easier to enter with eased regulations for foreign companies. South Korea has high-speed, aggressive local competition. Some companies make Australia the first entry point into Asia and then try to serve other markets from there. I've never seen it work effectively.

5. Frontier markets. Test a large, emerging market of the BRC: Brazil, Russia, and China. These markets take a long-term investment in what are now highly competitive local environments. Don't go there until you are satisfied with how the other markets have performed.

6. China is tricky and the most competitive market in the world. Unless you have a lot of money or political clout—which often go together—or a very trusted backer with deep China ties like Sequoia Capital, or a partner like China Mobile, I'd suggest steering clear. That said, Taiwan is much easier and has many more laws and trust working with American companies. Consumers are very technically savvy, perhaps due to the history of the semiconductor and contract manufacturing business across the island. An excellent way to work in China is to start in Taiwan and then expand with the help of the Taiwanese. Taiwan can be a conduit to China.

7. Southeast Asia/India. This archipelago is exploding with billions of people moving out of poverty. Each country has different regulations and acceptance of foreign companies. Albeit a small market, Singapore is a great launchpad into these territories. You can place a representative there to figure out which market fits your business best while selling into Singapore.

Use this spreadsheet as a reference.

International Analysis

Scan the QR code to view this
information as a spreadsheet.

HOW TO ENTER A NEW GEOGRAPHY

International expansion is risky and uncomfortable but can be wildly
profitable if done correctly. Flush with capital and staffed with global
citizens, well-funded startups can extend worldwide at the speed of
light but not with any certainty of success. Startups run by young rene-
gades burn through contacts and opportunities due to arrogance and a
lack of cultural understanding. Others too risk averse barely break even
with the help of a local partnership. Those who succeed have a sharp
discernment, protecting their downside while making a few educated
bets. Here's how to do it.

The Ways to Enter

There are several ways to enter a market: follow your customers (which
we covered above), go it alone, partner up, or start a joint venture. Err,
scratch that. There are only three. Most joint ventures (JVs) aren't
needed and don't work. JVs have too many conflicts, and it's a night-
mare to exit unless you accrue huge profits on your balance sheet. If
you're able to do a successful JV, you've probably already got a massive
company and don't need much help going international anyway. That
leaves two, which is now just a matter of sequencing.

Ideally, enter the market on your own to learn the landscape. Lacking feet-on-the-street experience, it's hard to make decisions from afar.
For this reason, send someone from headquarters to check out the landscape first, then hire a local salesperson or a market-entry representative—either a person or firm—in the target country. It's a good idea to

build relationships with multiple partners to familiarize yourself with the landscape. Once your presence is known, you can plant seeds locally. You might even find that other companies start approaching you. That's when the landscape knows you and...

That's when to get your feet wet. You can start your business through simple, nonexclusive revenue share sales and distribution agreements. By working with several foreign partners, you can vet out the committed ones. Your partners may want market exclusivity, which you should consider. Often, there isn't much sharing in many of these global markets, so by default, a nonexclusive deal with a partner may become default. Just don't sign an exclusive deal unless the partner performs. The answer: go at it alone, then partner up.

How to Pick a Partner

Strategic alignment. Financial. Culture/Values. Triangulate those and you'll have chosen well.

Sharing the same vision for how to invest and expand into the market is vital for success. The partner must understand your vision, be willing to replicate it in their market, and position it appropriately—with a few minor tweaks. You'll be confronted with a myriad of questions such as whether to work with an established partner or a smaller, hungrier partner, or whether to work with a market leader or a general investment firm. Whichever way you go, make sure the vision aligns.

Just as married couples must have agreed on a financial plan, so must you and your partner. Set a budget together and agree on spending ahead of time. They should also have skin in the game, either investing their own resources for localization or actual capital. Even better, look for a partner who wants to invest in you. Note: It's best for them to invest in the parent company that gives them ownership in the vision of the company. Investing in a separate local entity is essentially a JV, which offers little long-term equity value. Their financial commitment to your firm cements the alignment of interest. Just be sure not to take any investment prematurely, as that might preclude other, better partners from working with you. Being in financial harmony aligns risk and return.

Foreign cultures have a myriad of nuances. Hence, it's tough to align cultures of foreign subsidiaries. I often find myself asking the question, "What does company culture mean—is it the food they eat, the communication style, or dedication measured by working hours?" Default to values. Anyone anywhere can buy into clearly defined values of your company. It seems that Amazon's value system has been one reason it's built such a globally united workforce. Values transcend culture in a disbursed global workforce.

Know When to Double 'Em, to Hold 'Em, and to Fold 'Em

Before you open shop in a new country, you should create terms to measure your success. A good rule is to strive to achieve top-line growth in two years, but know that profitability will likely take another year or two. If you don't get revenue growth in year two, then are you making significant headway with partnerships? Are you learning enough about the market that you can justify another year or two of investment? Barring any of those results, it may be time to exit or to analyze your options. On the other hand, if you find a good partner and it's paying off, double down. As your confidence and chance of success increases, increase your bet by increasing human resources or making an acquisition. Know the KPIs that determine success, then decide to double 'em, hold 'em, or fold 'em.

TWO EXAMPLES OF INTERNATIONAL ROULETTE

Example 1—Place Small Bets in Several Markets

Apple needed 10 markets in Asia and we had minimal budget to execute. We placed small bets in each market by hiring local consultants in Japan, Singapore (Southeast Asia), Greater China (including Hong Kong and Taiwan separately), Australia, and India. We had people in Shanghai, Hong Kong, and Taiwan to have representatives covering the three different Chinese cultures and territories.

Betting on Greater China and Taiwan was risky. Taiwan was low on Apple's priority list due to its small size, but it was on Google's top-five gaming billing market. Coupled with that information and personal knowledge of having worked in Taiwan with gaming companies in a previous life, I knew the opportunity there was almost on par with Japan. In fact, it was greater than what we could expect in China, where competition and regulation was fierce, and in Southeast Asia, where user spending was minuscule. In the end, we were able to close similar telecom deals in Taiwan, and those carriers then told Apple of our leadership in the country. Taiwan succeeded wildly in becoming a top-five market for Boku. Hong Kong also outperformed expectations, while China was blocked out, as expected. Placing several small bets reduced our portfolio risk and increased our chance of success.

Example 2—Work with a Small, Hungry Partner
An example of this is when Twitter entered Japan in 2008. At first, they partnered with a leading Japanese incubation firm, Digital Garage, and allowed Digital Garage to adapt and market the product uniquely. Digital Garage created a custom Japan-only site, Twinavi, to help first-time users and bloggers understand the experience. To attract users, they also launched Twitter's first banner ad campaign anywhere in the world. Junichi Fujimoto, who worked for Digital Garage at the time, said, "The most significant uptick in users came from people preinstalling the Twinavi API and client on SoftBank mobile devices." Fujimoto-san now does separate market entry work for startups. Please contact me if you'd like to discuss with him.

This is a perfect example of how to start with a small, local partner and then scale effectively to even larger partnerships.

CHAPTER 8

STARTUP CORPORATE DEVELOPMENT

"Acquiring and integrating companies is undoubtedly a competitive advantage."

—KD's novice advice to Boku executives Mark Britto and Jon Prideaux

Startup corporate development may strike you as a juxtaposition of corporate activity in a startup world. It is. Corporates protect their existing businesses through acquisitions; startups can jump-start or enhance their fledgling businesses through acquisitions. Early-stage funded startups may not have considered corporate development as a strategic variable, but this perception is changing, especially for any startup looking to leapfrog their competition early in the race.

Boku made acquisitions almost yearly. The last player to enter a very crowded, fragmented field of over 20+ global competitors, Boku had to scale fast. Most of the players operated at or below their marginal cost—they were just treading water. That led us to realize that the one with the biggest balance sheet could win. Even with a small amount of funding, the company made two acquisitions right out of the gate that propelled it to a top-three position. Then, after a three-year hiatus and with a bigger pocketbook, the executives renewed the acquisition strategy to cement its position, buying companies and assets in India, Germany, and Italy. That strategy made Boku the clear market leader.

Even if you aren't the vanguard in the market, startup mergers can help you surpass your competitors. If you are a vanguard, it will keep you several boat lengths ahead of the others. Don't do this, and you risk treading water with the other also-rans.

Here's how: consider mergers and acquisitions (M&A). Make it part of your strategy by prepping your team and analyzing deals like a banker, then execute deals methodically.

Consider M&A Early in the Game

Because of the increase in venture capital worldwide, scaling a business globally through organic means has become nearly impossible. Within weeks of launching in Silicon Valley, startups may see clones pop up not just at home but also around the globe in China and Europe. This activity creates a fragmented market with many competitors, creating a confusing choice for potential buyers. For these reasons, just like international expansion, corporate development is something you must do to lead the pack and cross the second chasm to partner with a trillion-dollar tech company.

Be forewarned: it's not an easy move. M&As are among the trickiest moves a company can make. Political games, power struggles, cultural differences, and product integrations can easily derail the post-deal success. With a bang, M&As require two distinct and often competing companies (who were likely competitors before) to get along and work together. The only ones safe are the executives; everyone else is under the gun. In addition, integrating disparate technology into a single platform can throw product cycles into a frenzy. That's a lot of chaos. But if you can learn to manage this, you can create an unmatched competitive advantage.

Startup companies can create a winner-takes-all market out of the gates. Look at Elon Musk and Peter Thiel, for example. When gridlocked in the market, Musk and Thiel combined their payment startups to form PayPal, which ultimately made them billionaires. Sequoia Capital makes this an integral part of their startups' strategy. In a more recent Sequoia example, Mmhmm raised capital and bought a competitor, Memix, blocking them from taking share and a solidifying a winner-takes-all market. Otherwise, Memix may have been funded and become a pesky competitor. Make it part of your strategy early on, and you too may win the market by default. (Timing of M&A deals is even more critical since the government is now looking at antitrust with a keen eye. The earlier you acquire in a nascent market, the better.)

Make It Part of Your Strategy

M&A can take a lot of time, so don't dabble in it. As your company grows, bankers and other corporate development leaders will become interested in talking to you, to either buy their companies or be bought by them. When this happens, you'll need to talk with your investors and create an internal team of BD, finance, and legal services to assess potential deals. Most deals won't go through, and the last thing you want is for an M&A to distract your day-to-day operations. If you decide to do it, do it right. Prep your team early, get 'em talking, and analyze deals like a banker.

PREP YOUR TEAM EARLY

Yes, that's right: make another deal team. Holding deal reviews every two weeks will keep you on your toes. To do this, make a scorecard or sheet, and assign each M&A a simple high-, medium-, or low-ranking score for each of about 10 characteristics that include things like market size, market growth, competitive landscape and intensity, and revenue and gross margin profile. Once you've done that, you can look at the more intangible "fit" variables—the M&A's fit with core strategy, ease of product integration, the quality of new capabilities, cultural similarities, expertise in the management team, and so on. Make a small team of a few people to assess these deals early.

Get the board on board. Preparing them staves off questions and doubts about why you are buying companies when they thought they invested in the so-called clear market leader. Remember, venture capitalists want to deploy MORE money in successful companies, so they will load up your bank account if you compel them. Make sure you present them with clear reasoning and pricing scenarios for these acquisitions, and you'll have funds to deploy.

GET 'EM TALKING

The first step to initiating a merger or acquisition is obvious: get your people talking. To approve the deal, executives and board members need to foster relationships. In addition, having an open line with the higher-ups is vital to creating clear escalation plans.

Ideally, you'll already be working with the target company and know their team and synergies. The more you know ahead of time, the better. That said, sometimes you need to move quickly and just own the assets to get in the market leadership position. If this is the case, don't dilly-dally around.

Starting the conversation around M&A is easy—it's all about getting to the right person. Ask your BD lead to talk to their counterpart at the target company: "I'm just the guy from the cheap seats. Do you think we could get the CEOs talking?" (You can adjust the level of folksiness as you see fit.)

ANALYZE DEALS LIKE A BANKER

From 2001 to 2005, I painstakingly labored to pass three levels of the chartered financial analyst (CFA) exam. What I took from the certification was that to analyze acquisitions and make individual stock bets, you'll need a lot of spreadsheets and market assessments. M&A assessment is no different, and you cannot follow an ad hoc, fly-by-night approach. In essence, this section is about due diligence, and that process focuses on how to optimize synergies between the two companies. Here's how to convince your investors.

Quantitatively, financial modeling is vital to find your revenue and cost-saving synergies. Sometimes these things are super obvious, but sometimes they're not. Looking at high-, medium-, and low-success cases can help you develop your measures and get them approved at the board level. A good tip is to keep your modeling practical and easy to understand. Years ago, I learned the Monte Carlo simulation, which is highly complex and impossible to think through. By contrast, Warren Buffett uses a scratch pad for his investments. Find something in between.

Qualitatively, assess each transaction by how it fits with your company's course to a lighthouse, and how the M&A could fill your gaps. Do market research to look at geographic expansion, technology advantage, or desired customers. This information will help you create a list of acquisitions that could help you leap ahead with a talented team or unique technology—two key reasons to do a deal.

In an interview with Brian Isleib, technology finance and corporate development leader, he boiled it down to simplicity and clarity. During this process, entertain and dismiss ideas that range from the "mild" to the "wild." When you do, ask yourself the following questions about an acquisition primarily focusing on market position/presence, product fit, and revenue/cost synergies. (Again, strategy boils down to market positioning and product fit.)

1. **Market presence**—Does it consolidate the market early, making me the clear leader? Does it give me a new geographic presence? Are you in a stalemate? (You have some big customers; they have others. No one is switching.) Let your opponent know, "It may be better to work as one instead of beating each other up."

2. **Product**—Does it give me access to a new technology that can be used to tweak or pivot into a new market? Do I need a completely new line of business?

3. **Human resource**—Does it bolster my bench, giving me more engineers or talent?

4. **Revenues**—Does it make me the clear market leader through new revenues and customer acquisition? Is it defensive against my clients? (This is unlikely at this point but still worth asking.) Is it an arbitrage situation? Can I buy their revenues/profits at a low valuation relative to mine? Please visit www.kdalive.com for a due diligence checklist.

Due Diligence Checklist and Q&A Form

Scan the QR code to view this information as a spreadsheet.

Execute Deals Methodically

Once you've completed the due diligence, then execute the deal. This is the nuts and bolts of the deal. Here is a systematic way to get it over the finish line: deal process, terms, and structure; then the hard part: integration.

DEAL PROCESS AND STRUCTURE

Initially, keep the deal team small. Once you have a term sheet in place, you'll need internal support from all levels of your company to figure out the revenue synergies, cost savings, and product integration of the deal. More importantly, you need to get their buy-in so that after the deal, you integrate with ease. Dropping a whale onto your business leaders' laps will throw them overboard. Furthermore, you don't want to distract employees from day-to-day activities or worry if the news about the transaction leaked, so complete confidentiality outside of your deal team is essential. Keep it small and on the down low.

A deal's value is very subjective, so you may need to use your sales skills to convince your counterpart to commit. My best advice is to have an agreed-upon, logical framework of value for the two parties so both feel it's a reasonable deal. One example could be a ratio of sales with consideration for market growth potential. Another may be a human resource calculation, such as a ratio of the number of engineers. (Just shows you how much market power engineers have.) It may just come down to what you are willing to pay for it.

The BD team can negotiate the financial terms, but it helps to involve legal to arrange the structure. The most basic deal structure may be management lock-in. You can do this by vesting, meeting certain thresholds/delivery items, and offering a bonus for an earn-out. Mark Britto shares his thoughts on startup M&A:

> On M&A, the founder/CEO needs to internalize that stakeholders' interests are not always aligned. The board represents shareholders and not employees. The CEO needs to consider the benefits of shareholders and employees while considering the

outcome the acquirer (including management and shareholders) seeks. Depending on the capital structure, it's not unusual to have multiple classes of shareholders with somewhat divergent interests. To negotiate this complexity, take counsel from sophisticated outside advisors.

The acquirer is looking to buy assets, technology, and IP and retain employees more often than not. For employee retention, cash or equity stay-on bonuses are customarily negotiated. The buyer typically gives retention equity, coming in the form of options or restricted stock units (RSUs) with a vesting schedule. Another way to ensure retention is to hold back equity. Typically, 10–15 percent of the deal's purchase price is held back for 12–24 months against contractual claims. This holdback acts as an incentive for employees to stick around.

Tech and talent M&As are usually less complex and more successful than so-called mergers of equals (which a business union never is). Consider just buying the company's assets or making an acqui-hire (basically, employing the company's employees)—this is legally easier than purchasing the entire company. Keep it as simple as possible.

INTEGRATE TO STABILITY

Once you've made an M&A, your next challenge will be to integrate your technology and teams. The deal leader must work closely with the CEO to rearrange the organizational chart and integrate teams. Doing so is a function of clear organizational roles, communication, and culture. It's best not to dance around. Quickly assign new roles and establish direct reporting lines. The last thing you want is to throw the existing team off their current path or demoralize them by perceived demotions, so allow them to keep ownership of the task on hand. (Note: I generally don't suggest acquiring a company and promoting the other management team, but this *can* be a way to remove existing team members who you don't want around without firing them. Trust me, I know.)

First, Focus on the Organizational Roles and Responsibilities

What's paramount to create a stable outcome is to define who's doing what. There are operational expenses and time-to-market issues that arise with all M&A. How well you do this will affect your ability to take market presence or establish that market fit you're seeking. So plan it! Your goal is to manage this process until it becomes a fully integrated unit: technology, customers, finance, and team.

Your first step in integration is to assign an internal head who will form a team to lead the integration process. The team should consist of four leaders: technical, revenue, finance, and HR/organizational lead. Have one person overseeing the four leaders.

Technology integration and your roadmap are the most critical factors to the success of a transition. The tech leader integrates the product roadmap and convergence of the technologies. Depending on the platforms, APIs, and customer set, this can take years to do effectively. In doing so, prioritize customers and how to merge the technologies seamlessly for them or, in an undesirable circumstance, migrate them to a new technology. Either way, it's essential to get on the same page with the revenue leader to maximize customer synergies and limit customer churn.

The revenue leader is someone from the customer success team who will merge your customer sets. Transitioning existing customers and acquiring new customers rests on your ability to execute deals smoothly and timely. The revenue/finance duo must assess which technology is superior, merge roadmaps, and prioritize customers to retain.

The finance leader must join the charter of accounts, select an enterprise resource planning (ERP)/accounting system, and work closely with the revenue lead. Finance must make sure all customers receive on-par treatment and pricing. A good integration plan is also needed to keep the back office tight. Ensure that you can continue to close the books and report to management and the board. Missing blocks and tackles, the fundamental parts of the deal, will throw your team into disarray.

Second, Overcommunicate

If you don't, your entire company will rapidly start flailing about. Keep both parties up to date on the integration plan, both positives and negatives (such as layoffs). Your original employees may be uncomfortable with these changes, so be open with your team about what is going on. Being too secretive causes skepticism in the crew. To promote unity and align communication, we spoke as if we were one company, so we didn't address two separate companies. We did this by addressing each company—the existing and acquired—as "Your Company Name (India)" or "Your Company Name—Orange." Be consistent from day one. By keeping the team name the same and removing the different labels, you'll bring people together. Rearranging the organization chart is time consuming and emotional, so communicate often.

Third, Gel the Cultures

Effectively merging the culture/values gels teams. First, set a precedent; then make it collaborative. Since *you* are acquiring *them*, it's better for you to be the exemplar. It's not a one-way street, however. You may find some best practices that you'd like to incorporate from the other organization. Let's be real, what you really want is for people to get along and work well together. The only way to do that is to bring them together. Do this through skills training, team building, and work retreats. At Boku, we often held small group retreats. We once did a personality assessment and large scavenger hunt in Berlin. After an acquisition in India, we held a planning session in Singapore with some tourist activities like cooking. Letting people connect in a stress-free and fun environment builds lasting bonds and unifies teams.

Time spent on integration often comes at the expense of homegrown innovation, but it's necessary and worth it. Acquisitions can fill the gaps faster than any homegrown technology. Once you've gone through your first M&A, all subsequent acquisitions become easier. If you can acquire better than anyone else in your field, well, that's a clear competitive advantage. Get your integration team ready because executing the deal isn't even half the battle.

THE FLIP SIDE: USE CORPORATE DEVELOPMENT TO HELP BUSINESS DEVELOPMENT

M&A goes both ways, and it's essential to sniff around the corporate M&A offices of potential acquirers—just in case. Learn about their organizational charts, and network inside their organizations with a keen eye about the company mission and financial and operational goals. Your goal is to get the executives talking and find a sponsor who supports working with your company and pushing your agenda forward. Spending this time poking around can reap many intangible benefits and maybe result in BD deals.

Work from top down and within the organization. Since a firm hand is required to shake things up, start from the top when beginning a deal. Internal politics are daunting, and you don't want to be part of them, but you need to work through them. A C-suite introduction may intimidate some business leaders, so be friendly and unthreatening. They may feel threatened by the disruptions to their plans. You'll need to work these branches the hardest by talking up the M&A's value to them or by crafting a story of minimal harm. They, not the CEO, must be sold on your value. Still, it's good to have the CEO's eye looking down.

How do you get the CEO's attention?

There are several ways. One is to get your investors to help find the right contacts. The other is to hire a banker if you can. The last way is to let key people at companies know that your company may be looking for a strategic partner, and you'd like to have an initial call with relevant folks. By taking yourself out of the equation, it saves face for your contact. The last-ditch effort is to get to know the CEO's executive assistant and make friends until they give you a channel. That's a tip I learned from a sports rainmaker in London, Ricky Paugh, who runs 1440Sports. Take whatever measures you must to get not just the CEO's oversight but also his blessing.

HOW IT WORKS IN PRACTICE

Here is one example. In 2011, PayPal acquired our main competitor Zong, so Boku thought it would be an opportune time to put itself up for sale. Ron met with high-level executives from several of the global financial services and technology companies. His pitch wasn't about selling the company, though. It was about partnering for deals—with the unvoiced hope of an acquisition. The BD meetings piqued the interest of multiple partners and led to subsequent M&A meetings with bankers and the like. Although an M&A deal never worked out, the process led to several BD deals and one of Boku's biggest customers, Spotify.

After Boku, Ron worked at DocuSign, a unicorn SaaS company. Based on that experience, he notes, "In the early days, it's helpful to get sponsorships and high-level introductions at the organization. However, the real work comes from grinding it out with the team members who'll get value from the product and execute the deal. As a larger company, we'd do deals with smaller companies to explore their fit and use BD as a funnel for investment and M&A."

Companies are bought, not sold. More times than not, companies buy other companies they know well and with whom they have worked. Engaging executives through corporate development will catalyze BD processes that could lead to more lucrative outcomes.

The Impact of Boku's Mergers

In the fall of 2009, Boku wasn't just losing against our competitor Zong; we were getting decimated. In six months, I had managed to land only one deal. Making matters worse was a new entrant called Paymo. Paymo had a broader geographic reach than either Boku or Zong and gained the attention of big customers like Hi5 and Facebook. In addition, both Zong and Paymo had more extensive coverage than Boku, and both had a long history in telecom services.

We already knew where we fell short and how we could jump ahead. Our CEO, Mark Britto, asked me what we needed to do to win more deals, and it was glaringly obvious; we needed more geographic markets and a better product. It didn't take Mark long to deliver. He acquired Paymo. Ron led the product team to integrate the product in less than six months. Soon after, we ran the table and closed every deal on our list—nearly 36 weeks of one newly closed deal each week. With so many deals, we caught the attention of EA, Facebook, and Riot Games, leading to a significant turning point for the company. If you execute M&A before your competitors, you'll eat them and not be eaten.

WHAT NOT TO DO

Here is an example of what not to do. Don't get caught sleeping. Early on at Boku, we had the opportunity to acquire a peer-to-peer short message service (SMS) transfer company. A colleague and I spent about thirty minutes talking it over with the CEO, and we decided to pass. The company seemed exciting but tangential to our business. What we overlooked was that both our companies utilized SMS technology to transfer money—they between people, and we between companies. The company we passed up was Venmo, which now resides on 75 percent of smartphones in the United States.

Whether Boku could have made the acquisition is unclear; exploring our synergies further might have revealed how to offset our slow-moving customer traction. After that miss, I pushed our team to turn a keen eye to making acquisitions a part of its strategy. It took a few years of convincing, but we finally did. If you decide to do it, dedicate the time and resources to it. Focus on the synergies, and you won't miss any ships passing in the dark.

Several years after the Paymo deal, we were treading water, so we resumed our acquisitive strategy. While working on our lighthouse deals, we became aware that we needed more of a global footprint, particularly in Asia. Needing both a presence to show we were serious about winning the region and operational and technical support locally to service our customers, we acquired a small Indian firm, Qubecell. That acquired market presence and leadership earned the attention of Apple and Google India. We didn't stop after that.

Not all our acquisitions fared so well, though. After Boku became a larger company with a clear vision, navigating to the lighthouses, we acquired a nearly equal-size competitor in terms of employees, in Germany, to consolidate our forces in Europe. At large, it was a defensive move to keep them out of our biggest clients. It was a controversial decision as we were on the cusp of closing a very large client that would greatly impact our revenues. Presuming we had to protect our customer base, we made the bet. Combining two competitors threw the company into turmoil for some time. Trust me, it got ugly when we put salespeople together who'd been competing for a long time. Fortunately, Boku was able to get itself back together and recover—I didn't.

Since then, Boku has continued to acquire companies almost yearly, cementing its leadership in the space and markets around the world. It's worked marvelously for them.

CHAPTER 9

GALVANIZE YOUR CREW FOR TEAM SALES

"It's tough for one person, running solo, to close a big deal. They'll constantly harass the other side to the point where it's overwhelming. Ideally, you need three to five touch points into the organization with minimally, the business development lead, a junior salesperson, a product/technical manager, and executive support."

—Emil Michael, former Chief Business Officer of Uber

Incidentally, selling together was something we did naturally at Boku. We used to joke with each other around reciting Glengarry Glen Ross's "ABC—Always be closing." That wasn't our mantra, however; our mantra was "ABS—Always be selling." In the early days at Boku, no one was closing anything, so we *all* had to sell. We enrolled anyone in the company who wanted to help sell to friends, old colleagues, and to whomever we could get a meeting.

Here is an example of how we started co-selling. Right when the company started, I began to test co-selling with our VP of Customer Success, Nicholas Reidy (whom you'll hear from in Chapter 12). We'd go to conferences and meet different people at the same company. Afterward, we'd alternate pinging them. Nick would do so in a very informal, easygoing manner, while I'd follow up on the deal. The back-and-forth helped us gauge the timing and needs of the target company; it also allowed me to distance myself from harassing my contact, knowing that Nick would ping them every other time. As time went on, we crystallized this method and involved other team members. It became the foundation of our success and a core competency of the company.

Although your BD leader may be the captain of the ship, he can't do it all. He needs an entire crew to navigate through stormy seas to the lighthouse. To do this, the captain must involve different team members.

How do you get their enrollment? Simply, win together. Winning at team sales comes down to exciting your team, defining clear objectives and ownership, swarming the org, and following RFP best practices. Master that, and every deal is yours.

Excite the Team

With your deal plan in hand, it's time to organize the team. The BD Captain is not and cannot be a do-it-all. As the deal progresses, prospects will ask more precise questions. If the BD head pretends to be an expert and misses an item, it's going to reflect poorly on them and the company. Motivate your team to support the BD lead, and you won't miss a beat. Here's how I did it.

It started off the hard way. Once when I responded to a question a CTO asked me, he just chuckled and said, "I threw you a softie and you missed. Why don't we chat with your engineers?" Embarrassment humbles the ego. He was right. I could not be the spokesperson for all Boku's different functions.

I then became a messenger for the product and engineering teams. Sitting with the product and engineering teams at length, reading specification documents, and compiling that into sales vernacular, I obviated my ignorance. The more I did this, the more time I needed from other members on the team. This process became time consuming and inefficient. But I needed to do it.

I wanted them more involved in the deal. Instead of asking for parts of their time, I wanted lots of it; I excited them about being part of the team that won the deals. So I asked them to join the in-person sales meetings. Most were excited to shake up their day jobs in front of the computer. I got them to buy in.

Once the team was on board, I gave them the lay of the land and prepared them for meetings by offering tips on presenting, Q&A, and general salesmanship. Many were excited by the idea of rehearsing, speaking, and learning new skills. Even more fun than that, they got out of the office to meet others at top-tier firms. This new responsibility motivated and excited them about being part of the sales team and helping the company win.

The single most influential task your team will have is creating a shared vision. Forget selling to your client; sell to your team, and they will help you with the rest. Once again, set objectives.

DEFINE CLEAR OBJECTIVES AND OWNERSHIP

Setting objectives and giving ownership to members—generally a good management practice—clarifies working responsibilities and deliverables. Focus on four goals: matching organizational structures, ownership, presentation, and streamlined communication. Do that, and you won't get lost leading a BD team. Any way you look at it, each person has clear objectives and ownership of their material. The BD leader always captains the ship, so streamline communication back to him/her. Let's get into the weeds.

First, Know Your Counterparts

It's worth doing some organizational research before reaching out to a company. Doing some LinkedIn research beforehand sets the playing field. Even better, get an organizational chart from that prospect's company. One of my favorite moments at Boku was when a colleague called a meeting, pulled out what looked like a folded oceaneering map, unfolded it many times, and said, "Let's pick our people." It was the complete organizational chart of a division of one of our prospects and included well over 100 people. I don't know how he got it, but it was a vital document that helped us reach the right people in their organization.

Second, Peer Up and Tier Up

Once organized, peer up and tier up with your potential client's deal team, meaning, match job functions and seniority. The BD lead isn't

the only one who's keeping in constant contact with the potential partner. Make other employees follow up for coffees and meetings with
the target company. These meetups are great ways to check in on the
deal's impact across business functions. You'll often have no idea what's
going on with the other side unless you ask. Asking can also prove
fruitful since different team members talking will give you a varied
perspective on how the deal is coming together. For example, a product
manager who asks the big company, "What can we do better?" will
get a response on how to improve the product for the customer. An
engineer who asks the same question will answer the technical aspects
of the product. A finance person will learn about payment terms. So
forth and so on.

Third, Ownership Empowers

Each person should know and prepare their content, including an
explanation of their domain, presenting their content, and responding
to questions in meetings. Ready all content ahead of time—even the
kind that's supposed to sound like it's off the cuff. Keep a repository of
questions that have been and might be asked. If you are still waiting for
the RFP, prepare for it by prepping your content beforehand. Empower
each person to do their part.

Everyone practices their part of the presentation. Team members
write out the talking points, jot down the expected questions, and then
give their presentations to the BD team in a meeting room. Have someone play the devil's advocate to ask everyone the hard questions. Practice the answers.

Train your product managers and engineers in the art of "yes, and,
or, because." The answer to questions on infrastructure should almost
always be "Yes, and the infrastructure is there; we can have that ready in
a few weeks," or "Yes, because we've built the appropriate technology to
cover for DOS attacks." With the right partner and enough time and
money, anything is possible. You never know when a no could be a deal
killer. Sometimes the most trivial details will weigh on the mind of your
prospect. It's better to never give a flat-out no. Prep your team before
they give a pitch.

Last, Streamline Communication

Streamline communications and discuss an operational flow that gets everyone aligned. Ensure you know who is working on what deliverable and when they will reach out. The specifics of what information you've shared affect positioning, deal terms, and contract negotiations. As the deal progresses, the lead BD member doesn't always have to make contact; in fact, it's good to channel information through different people. Just make sure to review your data as a team before sending it out. Alignment keeps the ship sailing smoothly.

As I've said before, the team must sell the same story. Ad-libbing your storytelling will get you into trouble and may even lose you a deal. Your deal could be set back by weeks by something as innocuous as a member of your customer success team talking to a friend at the prospect. Your contact won't know whether to believe you or the rumor they heard floating around their office. Good companies will continuously fact-check your story, so any misinformation puts the deal at risk. Getting this internal consistency requires work. Make sure everyone is on the same page.

Create escalation paths in case the deal goes awry. When something's tipped you off that the sales process has gone astray, leverage your team of advisors and investors to be a part of your pitch team pyramid and expand your pursuit of the deal. CEOs don't attend every meeting. VPs meet the VP or CEO, product team meets with product team, and so forth. Team members of every level need to mobilize. When the time comes to bring in the heaviest hitters, you'll already have an escalation path established.

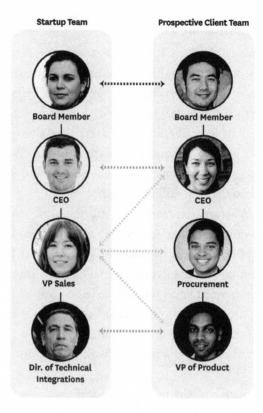

Startup Team   Prospective Client Team

Board Member   Board Member

CEO   CEO

VP Sales   Procurement

Dir. of Technical Integrations   VP of Product

Swarm the Org

As more and more team members at Boku became involved in selling, we won more deals. One by one, we saw the advantage of having several people on the deal team from all over the world. For example, while selling to Sony PlayStation, our core payments team was in California, but the deal sponsors were unknowingly in London. We didn't know that until we attended a conference at Mobile World Congress in Barcelona and met members of Sony Europe. After that, our GM of Europe built a relationship with the London team while I worked with the California team. We jointly sold the account, but if it wasn't for meeting the European team and forging a relationship with them, we might have missed our opportunity. In the end, the London team drove the deal.

This started a process I mentioned earlier called "swarming the org." In this process, we'd uncover a company's organizational structure and work on each of these contacts until we found the deal champion. Each team member remained in contact with their counterpart, consistently following up and maintaining the relationship. We were like bees all over a hive of honey.

Just buzzing around everyone at your lighthouse won't win you the honey, however. Adam Lee, Chief Product Officer at Boku, agrees that this was an effective tactic early in the sales process, but with the caveat that you need to add real value to the other company. Team sales at its best combine swarming the other organization with strong selling points; it is the clear tactical choice for landing a transformational deal. The first tactic is the RFP.

RFP Best Practices

It's best to prepare for an RFP well before it hits your inbox and you get overwhelmed. After receiving an RFP, you should create a deal alignment spreadsheet to keep track of each deliverable from every internal member. The spreadsheet reduces the number of redundant internal meetings you set up and clearly shows what needs to get done to execute the RFP. It also allows for ample writing and links out to more detailed diagrams or description.

The spreadsheet doesn't need to be aesthetically beautiful or show advanced business metrics and graphs. It has two purposes: communication and documentation. To make the best chart, only include material that fulfills both goals. Salesforce, RFP360, and Loopio are quality RFP software systems to check out.

Once the RFP arrives, this spreadsheet will evolve into a question-by-question action item list. Hopefully, your team will have prepared for most of these questions; otherwise, you may be scurrying around for a few weeks. Add the RFP sheets to your communication file as separate, numbered tabs, and label each Q&A interaction a team member has with its relevant RFP section.

RFP Best Practices

Scan the QR code to view this
information as a spreadsheet.

There will be plenty more RFPs after the first one, so keep a master RFP with every question you've ever received. Then an RFP merely becomes a copy-and-paste exercise. Here is an example of RFP topics:

1. Introduction
   a. Executive summary
   b. Overview and history
   c. Problem and your solution
   d. Competitive advantages
   e. Global footprint
   f. Diagram and flows
   g. Platforms/environments
   h. Technical overview

2. Finance
   a. Long-term customer value
   b. Business model, modeling, and ROI—work together
   c. Reporting

    d. Payment timing

    e. Reconciliation

    f. Dispute process

    g. Risk management services

    h. Taxes: international

3. Technical Deployment

    a. Sandbox testing

    b. Trial and phased rollout

    c. Onboarding plan

    d. Launch

    e. Post-launch

    f. Evaluation/KPIs

4. Support and Escalation

    a. Escalation paths

    b. Personnel

    c. Technical support

    d. Other support

    e. Education and updates

    f. Collaboration and resolution

5. Security and Risk

    a. Types of risk

    b. Unauthorized purchases

    c. Lost/stolen device

    d. Social engineering/malware

    e. Best practices

6. Service-Level Agreement

   a. Scalability

   b. System architecture

   c. Security

   d. Redundancy

   e. Technical, i.e., servers

   f. Reliability and uptime

7. Marketing

   a. Loyalty marketing, etc.

   b. Co-promotional support

Being thoroughly prepared for RFP responses is a competitive advantage. I can tell you this because both Sony and Apple told us our responses were far superior to the competition. You must organize the team and questions well in advance before you get it. That will make answering the questions much less stressful. As Mark Britto said, "Boku's competitive advantage was writing RFPs and raising capital."

How Boku Thrust into Team Sales

At Boku, our joint selling process (either with Account Management or other global sales members) evolved into an entire team process almost by force. I was sitting on the beach in Jamaica and got two emails about RFPs for Sony and Microsoft on the same day. *Seriously?* Two RFPs in one day—a day that happened to be one of my precious few days off? To be honest, I went into a significant, anxiety-fueled panic. Thankfully, we had a calm lawyer who settled my nerves and helped organize the process.

A few months later, we presented the RFPs. My contact at Sony prefaced it with "Don't screw it up," so the pressure was on. I knew I wouldn't be able to deliver all the necessary details, so I asked everyone in Boku's leadership group if they wanted to join the meeting and chat with Sony's team when the time came. Everyone agreed, and over the next month, we practiced our pitch together. More than 10 people on our side and a dozen from Sony's joined the meeting. We crushed the presentation and won Sony. That pitch prepared us for the Microsoft presentation, which occurred about three months later.

Building on our theatrical presentations at Sony and Microsoft, Boku delivered an encore at Apple about a half year later. Afterward, one executive commented, "Your team's depth was far superior to the others, and you showed up with ten people, while your competitors showed up with two or three. There was no question in our minds about your commitment and ability to execute."

Let me close with this. Cynics in the technology and business world will likely disagree with my emphasis on team sales, arguing that it's a waste of time for non-BD people and that a capable BD person should handle the deal process on their own. Why take so much time away from others if the deal isn't even confirmed? I won't say their cynicism is entirely misplaced but that it's part of risk management. If the risk tradeoff is there, it's worth it.

CHAPTER 10

MOVE THE MARKET YOUR WAY

"Let your PR do the selling for you by having your targets know who you are
and what you're about before you ever walk into a room."

—Gregg Delman, Founder of G Three Media

Everyone knows Steve Jobs could single-handedly move a market with
one swoop of his magic wand in front of a keynote slide deck. A case in
point is what he did with the first-generation iPhone. When the first
iPhone was released, several smartphones were already on the market
by Nokia, Motorola, Palm, and BlackBerry. These companies had deter-
mined that open-faced touchscreens didn't sell well, but Steve Jobs's
presentation selling the phone plus the app store convinced the world
otherwise. The iPhone, vis-à-vis Steve Jobs's keynote, won the market.
He was the show.

Take a page from Steve Jobs, apply it to the B2B space, and build up
enthusiastic responses from your customers with your pitches. By hosting events and utilizing public relations (PR), you can announce exciting new features, new customer adoption, acquisitions, and more. But
remember, it's not just the people roaming the conference floor you'll
want to thrill; your moves and marketing strategies need to enliven your
lighthouse account as well. Your message should be simple. "We are
credible, we have competitive advantages, and we are coming across
the chasm, so get on board." Moving the market depends on creating
an ambience of anticipation around your business. Thanks to Silicon
Valley marketing/PR executive Josh Wein and Gregg Delman, Founder
of G Three Media, a PR firm that works with many startups for their
contributions to this section.

He defines it step by step: the steps to make some waves and move the market your way are establishing credibility in the market, showing market leadership, and being relentlessly consistent with press releases and event appearances.

What's the Big Deal about PR?

All press is good press, right? Wrong.

PR serves many purposes for a startup, but it's not widely understood. Media attention raises awareness about your company or product, but this isn't traditional marketing where you invest $1 and get $1.15 back—and if it's bad press these days, then you are in the red. Press rarely translates into an immediate short-term appreciation of benefit. Therefore, to get a long-term return, your press must align with your BD strategy and build a strategic narrative over time. Executing this tandem is a far more difficult task than short-term, one-off releases. That's understood.

When done correctly, press works. With the right timing, consistency, and messaging, press releases *can* create credibility for your business and give you a perceived leadership position in the market. When you first get a press hit, you might see an uptick in traffic, inbounds, social media mentions, and all the other typical metrics. That's great in the short term. Over time, though, you'll start to notice other intangible benefits, such as people knowing who you are when you walk into a room. Hiring may become easier because people know your brand. Your inbound BD leads may steadily increase. The company esprit de corps can increase because the external world now recognizes you as a leader. At last, you'll know you are on a hot streak when the usual stream of contacts you get comes in more at the rate of a firehose than the trickle of a faucet.

Establish Credibility

The goal of the press is simple: to create a media profile that builds trust in your brand, your company's ability to execute, and a glimmer of light where you are headed. Wherever prospects look, they'll find the idealized picture of the company, which you have painted and disseminated across the internet.

CREATE THE STORY ARC

Reflect on the storytelling section and the ways you can manage change in your company's trajectory. There is no better way than PR. Gregg emphasizes that your press releases must tell the arc of your story over time, demonstrating your successes and indicating from where you have started to where you may go. Intertwining your account with the press manages the market's impression of you and gives you control. Many errors are made when PR doesn't consider your story arc, so look out to the future and make sure your arc goes up.

Stories in the media should reaffirm your credibility and demonstrate consistency. When the recipient of your cocktail speech types your company name into Google, info will pop up. If nothing comes up, it will look like your business has some severe advertising and SEO issues. The content they see should support everything you told them in your cocktail speech and preview your charted path forward. Your press releases should make clear the competitive advantage that separates you from your competition. Competitive advantages are often fleeting, but consistently leveraging and churning them out is a competitive advantage in and of itself. Keep your press releases up to date to show that you are an innovative company that embraces change. *Have no doubt: constant innovation creates credibility and leads the way.*

STORIES TO DISPLAY

Press releases are not limited to significant, company-changing events. There are multiple types of stories that will yield returns.

- **Financing**—A story about your most recent financing round provides confidence that you have the funds needed to execute your plans. It also signals to the world that smart money is on you. Cash crowns the king. Once the media buys into your

financing round, you can use that as an inroad to share your
story, advantages, and vision. In addition, establish relationships with reporters. The reporters who invest in you early will
follow your progress over time and will benefit from riding your
wave as well.

- **Closing**—A story about significant customer traction and how
  another customer has benefited from your solution can help
  speed a BD process up. You demonstrate that you can provide
  the service you are selling in a customer-centered story, and the
  press will also help other potential customers understand what
  you might do for *their* company. This story can be precious if
  you're selling new and unproven technology; such customer
  testimonials can go a long way in inspiring confidence.

- **Innovating**—A story about new product features and technology will plant you firmly in the market of the lighthouse
  account. If you can do something that others can't, your company automatically becomes desirable, and the market will
  yearn for more.

- **Acquiring**—A story about an acquisition in the market that
  represents your clear market leadership, geographic expansion,
  and financial strength builds trust. The press loves acquisition
  information. Give it to them as early as possible without leak-
  ing the story.

- **Hiring**—Use PR to recruit critical hires. A story about head
  count or HQ growth can demonstrate the business's overall
  health and reassure potential customers that you are here to
  stay. It can also signal an opportunity to those in the market
  looking for jobs.

- **Aligning internally**—Press releases also create visible guardrails
  for your team when discussing company business with people
  outside the company. If the information is public, team members know they have free rein to talk on the subject. Otherwise,
  your people should know they must keep it under wraps.

All of these points will help you close the lighthouse, and when you do, tell that story to mark your leadership in the field. A prominent partner will be eager for a news story that portrays them as a market leader. Offer to involve them in your PR to boost your mutual brands. Reporters seek meaty stories, so releases with impactful clients that delineate a market movement and innovation are good ideas.

These are all tactics that Ron, Gregg, and I have used. In the early days at Boku, we were very aggressive with PR and events, mainly to catch up with a first mover and cement our place in the market. We used PR to announce acquisitions and customer wins; for instance, we announced more than 10 new customers on the platform who provided references. Further down the road, we announced new product releases and features, hoping to lure a lighthouse to the table. We wanted to show that we had the market momentum and features they needed. Do this right, and the wind will blow your sails.

Lead the Market

Propel your company into market leadership. To do that, be very calculated about when and how you release information. Repetition, repetition, repetition will put you on the path to victory. Do it with dignity by making your releases exclusive. You'll know you are doing it right when you start to get inbounds from larger companies and leads from your friends in the market.

TIMING IS EVERYTHING

Some venture capitalists say not to reveal your competitive advantages ever. Competitors move quickly, and press releases invite targeted efforts to snatch up your customer base. Many companies don't even want to add testimonials from their biggest customers on their website. They also think that conferences are a waste of time since they pose the risk of information leakage. But there may be times to do it; timing is everything, right?

There is *some* truth to this way of thinking. It's always your competitors who pay the most attention to your press releases—far more than your customers, for sure. However, it's also likely your customers already know what you're about to announce. Your horse needs to be already out of the gates—the press release is that first kick to create separation between you and the competition, the kick that prevents you from falling behind while keeping the competition on the chase. Get out front and don't be ashamed to show your strength, but make sure you have your patents filed. Use press releases when you've already solidified one competitive advantage, then you're ready to work on building the next one.

REPETITION STICKS

Audiences best absorb and remember messaging when it's repetitive and recently consumed. You'll notice that official press releases can often sound repetitive, but this is not an accident. Think about a politician on TV or a lawyer giving a closing argument. They state the conclusion first, provide some details to back it up, and state the conclusion again. You hear the main point of their opinion first when you're most likely to be paying attention. Then you probably see it again in a boilerplate on multiple releases or in interviews, all in the same form to ensure you're picking up what they're putting down. Repetition, repetition, repetition. It's how we learn and how we retain information.

Don't stop during the dry times. Dry times are good times for reevaluating PR priorities, tweaking messaging, and looking for previously unthought-of opportunities to get your message out there. Your company won't have news in each of these categories all the time. Gregg mentions that a quality PR firm helps you think through what stories can be newsworthy. They will search for timely content that can be communicated to a larger audience. If a company is in a dry spell, PR can focus more on thought leadership pieces that correlate with the news cycle and offer content that augments the articles. News outlets don't always publish these requests, so make sure to utilize platforms like LinkedIn and Medium to get your word out there. This strategy serves to build brand awareness and bolster the personal brand of the C-level executive who gets the byline. Whatever you do, don't turn off the spigot.

PRESERVE THE INTEGRITY OF PRESS

Methodically rolling out your press preserves the integrity of the announcement. Let's reflect on the deal plan and team. It's vital for your deal team—that is, colleagues, advisors, and investors—to preserve the integrity of your news by keeping it under embargo until you're ready to announce. Make sure your investors don't add it to their LinkedIn, tweet about it, or do anything else to make company information publicly consumable. When it comes to fundraising, a violator of news is Form D, which must be filed 15 days after the sale of securities.

Tell your lawyers that they must check with you when they're about to file Form D, which tells the world that you've sold securities and raised X amount of dollars. Journalists love Form D, and they scour the public information to see how much companies are raising. There are ways around filing Form D (filing state by state, which doesn't necessarily publicly disclose that information), but just make sure you get your legal team's advice.

Do these three tactics—timing, repetition, and integrity—and you'll see your SEO hits skyrocket and a large influx of inbound leads. Not only that, but when your lighthouse accounts read the news, there will also be one bright light shining, and it'll be you.

Be the Show

Tying together conferences and PR is essential. As I said initially, you need to *be the show* at conferences, not just attend. You can't let on that you're an amateur, so don't act like one with a flyer and a small booth at the conference. Go big or stay home when it comes to conferences. There are several ways you can do this:

1. Make sure your PR overlaps with your BD efforts on the ground.

2. Buy a sponsorship that includes a speaking arrangement so you can showcase your thought leadership.

3. Email the conference organizers to get access to the editorial aspects.

4. Host exclusive dinners with up to two dozen clients.

By doing these things and creating your conference presence, you show market leadership and avoid being just another person wandering the floors, struck by wanderlust. You don't need the most expensive booth. Face-to-face opportunities give you the best chance to show confidence and know-how. Get access to the biggest speaking slots; the speakers hang out with other speakers to avoid the crazy pit-jumpers. Remember, my success rate at pit-jumping conference speakers was dismal—just 25 percent. If you want to add meaningful contacts to your network, get a speaking slot. Be the one everyone wants to talk to, not the one chasing everyone else around. Look and act like the market leader.

Post COVID-19, who knows when conferences will reappear. However, when they do, conferences will still reinforce your presence and a way to learn about your competitors. As a fringe benefit, conferences also work as a training ground for new employees to get out of the office and see what the revenue team is doing. Many venture capitalists say conferences are a waste of time, which may be true in the B2C startup. When entering a market, especially if you don't have significant venture capital backing, conferences help with visibility and leads. At the very least, it doesn't hurt to look around.

CREATE A DOMAIN EXPERTISE

Get them to call you by creating an expertise they need. Hounding your lighthouse isn't always comfortable or appreciated. A good way around this is to create a situation in which they need to call you. Perhaps you find a gap in their business that doesn't pertain to your deal but is in the same industry you occupy. If you're the domain expert, they may need to call you for advice. Let them, and use these conversations as an opportunity to build rapport, rather than always coming through the front door.

Collect and disseminate information. Survey people about their interests. Pump out industry newsletters and small research pieces. Ask people to contribute to a quarterly report that you share with the group. Position your business as a leader in knowledge. Keep the information flowing between parties, and you'll always be top of mind. Instead of you chasing them, they'll start coming to you.

HOST INVITE-ONLY EVENTS

Be the talk of the town and host events that people want to join. Especially at crowded conferences, small dinners act as a place of refuge. Don't do one-off events for the show because rarely does one event help you move the needle—it's more like an introduction. Use your domain expertise and be consistent in both theme and periods. There are a few ways to host events.

The most obvious one is self-serving events. Use them to put the nail in the coffin for a deal. Host small exclusive dinners with specific targets in mind. An example is a CEO dinner. Float the idea by saying something like, "I think the CEOs should get to know each other. Why don't we have a quorum, get a small group together to talk shop?" Or you can frame it as a meeting of the minds, like a whiskey-tasting event for top executives to trade notes. If everything goes well, you can bring together a few of your existing customers and your top lighthouse prospect. They'll discuss your company's benefits with the lighthouse—that is, let your customers do the selling for you. It's best when self-serving situations don't seem that way to others.

Another type is a broader, industry knowledge-sharing event. Make your business the one that looks like it brings leaders together. One way to do this is to host quarterly roundtable discussions. This entails inviting people to join a specific group that focuses on one segment of the market. At Boku, I organized a broad payments industry dinner even though our company was only a speck on the radar of that industry. It reaped enormous rewards for us. By creating a collegial atmosphere with other companies, we made friends in the market and shared information openly. The key to my success was that I made it clear that I wasn't trying to sell but was hosting to exchange ideas and best practices.

Here's what happened at Boku. Circa 2009 (seems like a long time ago, I know), the social games and mobile games markets exploded with many events. Showing a solid presence put Boku on equal footing, leading speaking panels made us formidable, and hosting dinners made us the favorite. This barrage of nearly two events per month continued for years until our market was saturated, exhausting us physically and mentally. We had to rethink a strategy to cross the chasm. At that point in 2013, we started focusing solely on exclusive dinners and roundtables.

At these exclusive events, Apple, Sony, Facebook, and other online game companies joined us and traded notes on payments. At one specific dinner, I invited a guy whom I thought was the most outstanding young payments analyst from an online games company, Riot. He dazzled everyone at the dinner with his knowledge of payments from Russia to Brazil. This man praised our company, albeit with a few critics, and his feedback convinced the big boys we were the top player. To this day, I think that dinner was the one that convinced Apple to invest in us.

How to Combine Marketing/PR with BD

Getting the product into the customer's hands with low barriers significantly shortens the sales cycle. Here is how to do this using a coupled PR and marketing promotion.

In an interview with David Maynard, former Manager of Mobile Applications at Box, he explained that in 2012, Dropbox was well established in the consumer space. Their business model provided some storage for free (up to some amount) and then charged consumers for additional space. Box focused on the slow-moving enterprise market. To acquire slow-moving customers more quickly, they launched a mobile application for consumers who would lead them into the enterprises they worked for. At the Mobile World Congress in Barcelona in March 2012, Box offered a free 50 GB of storage for life for anyone who signed up with the free Box Android application. It was an effective marketing and BD move that helped consumers adopt the Box mobile application and served as an entry point into enterprises. Box ended the promotion for new users after a year or so and acquired hundreds of new enterprise accounts. Coupling conferences and marketing promotions can reduce your barriers to adoption.

Use Marketing Promotions to Reduce Barriers to Adoption

Reducing barriers to adoption gets the product in their hands. Jason Spero, an executive at Google, worked at a startup called AdMob, one of the first mobile advertising networks, later bought by Google. Running a marketing promotion to get your product in customers' hands at a significant discount, even free, is a good strategy. Early on, we gave $1,000 of free advertising to publishers that signed up on the network. Offering this incentive did a few things. First, it created an incentive for publishers to integrate and invest in development coding. Second, it helped promote those publishers, who grew their user base and available inventory. And third, it put money into the economy for other publishers to earn. This marketing effort primed the flywheel of supply and demand. It also brought down barriers for larger companies to test out the product. Getting the product in their hands was a critical step in winning the deals.

Move the Market like Steph Curry Moved the Game

Let's compare PR/marketing to how Steph Curry re-created the NBA to play the game his way. We all know Steph Curry. Before his David-son College NCAA run his sophomore year, he was unknown. After that, he was on everyone's radar, but could he turn into a dominant force in the NBA? Because of his relatively short height and inferior speed and jumping ability, most people doubted him. For the three years of his career, he was an above-average point guard, working diligently on his game and averaging in the high teens. Then in 2012, he leaped in his scoring. And in 2013, he made a major breakthrough, scoring 24 points per game and winning NBA championships.

So what happened? Other point guards were fast and flashy, so he had to find a way to beat them in another way. "Curry forced the game to change, from the Charles Barkleys who believed you couldn't win trying to hit 3-point shots to those players who had to literally change the way they played to keep up."[11]

Steph Curry's off-season routine relentlessly focused on how to change his game and the game itself. He studied old films and games from the great point guards like Pistol Pete Maravich, Steve Nash, Isa-iah Thomas, Magic Johnson, Allen Iverson, and even his contempo-raries such as Dwayne Wade, Russell Westbrook, and Chris Paul. He rehearsed their moves, passes, and shots over and over. He then went to his core strength which was a fast release and pinpoint accuracy from the three-point line, which he extended to almost anywhere inside the half-court line. Why would anyone want to shoot farther out than the three-point line? That wasn't logical. If he could do it, though, everyone would have to play his game.

He redefined the game of basketball by stretching out the court. By doing this, he would then control the floor the minute he stepped over the half-court line and spread out the defense.

Opponents had to adjust to his game. Similarly, with PR and mar-keting, you can define your story, your market leadership, and the game. Make your opponents catch up to you, and you'll be the one to beat. The graphic below is credited to Kirk Goldsberry, @kirkgoldsberry on Twitter.[12]

Most Common Shot Locations in the NBA

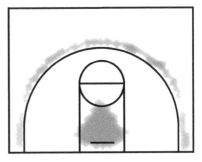

2001-02 (pre Steph Curry)   2016-17 (post Steph Curry)

CHAPTER 11

INTERNATIONAL TEAMWORK

"Coming together is a beginning. Keeping together is progress. Working together is a success."

—Henry Ford[13]

There is no competitive advantage better than a globally integrated team working in harmony. Building such a team doesn't happen overnight. It takes time to find employees across the globe whose vision and talent match yours. Once you've hired them, it takes even more time to build rapport and manage them. In the end, this time will be worth it. With your new global team, you'll be ready to woo your lighthouse accounts right off their feet.

Winning a deal with Sony and Apple required our teams to be in sync across the world. To win the Sony deal, we had our team in Japan, the United Kingdom, and the United States work together. Apple was even more extensive, involving members from India, Taiwan, Japan, Saudi Arabia, and Germany. The vision of executing the deal focused the company on executing something bigger than anything an individual office could achieve by itself. Uniting a global workforce relies on a shared vision and shared values, while respecting the diverse cultures.

To build a tightly knit global workforce, companies must articulate their visions and values, then work diligently to integrate and manage the teams. It's easier said than done because it takes time and effort.

Building Global Teams

The Silicon Valley adage is "hire slow and fire fast." I don't ascribe to this because only companies who are in the preferred position can hire slow. If I see the right fit, I'll pull the trigger quick. Internationally, however, the stakes are higher. Hiring people who can do the job and fit in with your company's cultures and values takes time.

Additionally, local hiring rules can make international hires more challenging. Few international markets include at-will employment like in California. In Germany, for instance, after a person is past their probationary time on a contract, it's difficult to fire them. Thus, in tightly regulated employment markets, it's advisable to send one of your staff overseas to get acquainted with the region before hiring. You need to understand your commitment to a person before handing them a job offer and the penalty to you if you decide to let them go.

Most foreign firms begin by hiring a country manager. Ideally, this person should possess native and bilingual speaking skills, relevant domestic and domain experience, and an international perspective, possibly with an overseas degree. At a minimum, this person should have a startup mentality and be a good cultural fit. I prefer someone with domain expertise, but I know others who've hired generalists who can pick up the technology quickly.

In an interview with Faissal Houhou, ex-Boku and Hyperloop executive and European BD expert, he said:

> The best quality to look for is someone who constantly knows how to navigate the market. In big companies and government, the network of decision makers changes, so bet on someone who is nimble and knows how to create a network from scratch versus people who proclaim that they have an existing network that will suffice. Startups change, and so does the network a business development person needs if they want to succeed.

In 2014, Boku hired Hiroshi Yoda. He had the perfect experience and adequate English but lacked an MBA and had never lived abroad. What set him apart was his experience working with overseas payments companies that had entered Japan—he understood the startup mentality. Within a year of being hired as VP of Business Development, Hiroshi helped Boku close deals on all the major telecom carriers, launched Sony and Apple in Japan, and was promoted to General Manager and now the SVP across Asia.

INTEGRATING THE TEAM

Successful companies snowball. A startup can grow from a small office in a technology incubator to a multinational operation in just a few years. Many entrepreneurs build technology but aren't experts in scaling and managing a global team. Here are a few principles to follow should you find yourself facing the lucky challenge of managing an international team.

Focus on People Integration

Integrate your foreign offices as you did acquisitions. Companies often underestimate the need to integrate their local team into a foreign country. Companies should have individuals at headquarters dedicated solely to working with and educating the home team about the foreign market, especially those markets where opportunity and barriers to entry are equally considerable in size.

Faissal Houhou continued:

> Encourage your overseas hire to stay at headquarters for one to three months (or at least visit for two weeks per month for three months) to get to know the people, the roles, the spirit, and the DNA of the foreign team. That way, when they are alone on the ground, they will have the knowledge and the internal support to handle any issue.

Have a United, Global Vision

A shared vision unifies people of different cultures, personalities, and temperaments. Your company may need to deploy slightly different strategies in each country where it operates, but everyone should be working toward the same goal. Boku's vision was to make the mobile number the world's most convenient way to pay online for digital content. To do this, not only did individual offices have to execute their part, but they also had to work internally to achieve the vision together.

Empower Offices Independently

Independent offices should be nimble and own decision making. The technology behind each transaction was different in Japan than it was in India, meaning we needed other development and resources in each market. Allowing teams to make independent decisions based on your company's unified vision will expedite execution. So long as everyone in the company is on the same page, the result in each country should be the same no matter the different means. To get the desired result, empower each office to make decisions.

Promote Consistent Values

Promoting the same values across the company fosters consistent approaches to thinking and processes across the company. Listing, sharing, and reinforcing values with the team is critical to creating a global company culture. Cultures drastically differ across countries. Values underscore how the company operates, communicates, and works together. Values transcend culture and unite.

Treat Employees as Equally as Possible

Living standards and salaries may vary widely by country, but vacation policies and work-from-home days should not. Holding employees accountable and rewarding them similarly, regardless of where they reside, creates a sense of equality. When employees in different regions are treated unequally, they may feel their contribution is less valued than others.

Maintain a Consistent Organizational Structure

Keep a similar organizational structure across different countries. Doing this can help employees communicate more effectively. Calling a team "Technical Account Management" in one country and their counterpart "Customer Technical Support" in another could confuse team members about their roles and positioning. Adding and budgeting for new functions worldwide will also be easier if the organizational structures are consistent.

Set Up Cross-border Reporting Lines

Create cross-border reporting lines to integrate employees around the world. Satellite employees should directly report to people with similar function in headquarters. This direct line of communication can help remote employees feel more like they're a part of the bigger team instead of isolated in their home country. For this reason, avoid creating a system where all employees report to the country manager who then reports to headquarters. Keep a balance of reporting lines between local and HQ. Otherwise, you run the risk of creating an unwelcome fiefdom that separates the organization and limits information spread. It can also result in high turnover in certain regions. Keep cross-functional, cross-border reporting lines in addition to local hierarchy.

Share Information Globally

Collect and share information across your organization consistently. This information sharing helps the company operate smoothly and can positively influence your strategic decisions. Employees in a satellite office may know about a unique technology or a local deal that, extended to the rest of the company, could be critical to success. Announcing company news to everyone at the same time creates trust with employees and puts everyone on the same page.

Even more important, create channels for sharing information during an emergency or critical event. What happens if there is an outage? What if a customer threatens to pull the plug or switches to a competitor? What if there is a pandemic or, even worse, a war? There is nothing worse than a barrage of emails with no person in charge. Plan so you can disperse information efficiently and effectively.

Enjoy Learning about Different Cultures

Treat the foreign markets you're expanding into as more than just financial opportunities. Strive to learn about each culture and the business culture of each country as well. In Japan, for example, it is customary for travelers to bring *omiyage* (gifts) or candy-like snacks to the office for others to share. At Boku, anyone who traveled abroad brought snacks to the partner office; anyone who traveled to HQ was taken to our favorite local restaurants when visiting. Another way to understand a different culture is to learn to speak their language or, at the very least, a few greetings. Learning about each other's culture creates mutual respect between individuals, builds relationships, and makes the integration and BD process much more human.

An Example of Global Integration Done Well, Boku-style

At Boku, we had offices in several locations. Our main headquarters was in San Francisco, and we had remote offices in London, Tokyo, and Singapore. Our teams worked well together and spent a lot of time building rapport. We trusted each other to fulfill whatever part of a deal we were working on. Without those strong relationships, we wouldn't have been able to close deals with lighthouse accounts in three different geographies.

One example of this was in 2011 when I worked with our General Manager of Europe, James Patmore. James and I were in London working on a technology deal with Sony. Unexpectedly, Sony asked if our technology was ready to be tested in the console environment. It wasn't yet—we didn't even have their tech specifications—so we asked Sony to clarify their requirements and said we'd get back to them pronto. Once the London team had Sony's specs, they passed it on to our San Francisco team. One of our product team leaders and an engineer worked all weekend to produce a custom document that fit Sony's technical specs exactly. The following week, Sony said it was perfect. That could only be done with a team united in vision.

A COLLECTION OF CULTURAL ADVICE

Becoming familiar with different cultures is one of the most fulfilling aspects of doing business globally. It's an integral challenge of global development since many cultures are quite proud of their way of doing things. I've seen inexperienced BD cowboys ride a unicorn from Silicon Valley to Japan and expect the Japanese to be at their beck and call. It didn't work. Let's look at a few countries that may fall into your priority list.

Europe versus the United States

There are some general differences between Europeans and Americans that are worth discussing. Europeans don't check emails on weekends, and they take six to eight weeks off on summer holidays—no matter the status of the deal. Another difference is that Europeans always respond to your messages, whereas we've got a large ghosting culture in the United States. I think these two points are something from which the United States can learn.

There are many differences within European countries, as Max Lehmann notes below:

> Knowing how to do business in each culture is essential before taking the plunge. Italians and Spanish want to hang out, wine and dine, and get to know each other that way, while the French go one step further and want to get to know your values and family. In the UK, brush up on your cricket, European history, and visit a pub or two. British like to poke into your general intelligence.
>
> Textbook Germans (Hamburg, Düsseldorf, and Berlin), on the other hand, are more transactional and analytical; following the hierarchy and process is a must, or else. They would not go to dinner before the deal was completed. However, in Bavaria—where I come from—we like a good biergarten and Oktoberfest celebration with our partners. In the Nordics, many are consensus-driven; you may need to convince five people in the room. Before you go anywhere, understand the processes of each culture.

Germany

In one example, a German games company had a bidding process that included only one round of offers. Max tried to work several angles of the organization but ended up offending the deal champion—he had disrupted the internal process. He ended up losing the deal to a local company. (Germans are very prideful and loyal to local companies. They also toe a line on their internal processes.) Also important, Germans are very detailed and require the facts—proof, statistics, and figures—to make a business deal. They prefer working with established and safe technologies and are highly concerned about data privacy.

The United Kingdom

Mark Gerban, an American business executive who's spent a lot of time in Europe, has his own experiences. He says, "In the UK, it's not professional or kind to be direct. People build themselves up to be highly qualified and of importance primarily because of their hierarchical culture. Just make sure they can walk the talk. Take them to a pub and find out what they are made of."

I found the British way of talking around things uncannily similar to the Japanese—maybe it's the "everyone knows everyone" island culture. Both cultures respect and speak indirectly. To get the Brits to fancy you, brush up on your Churchill history, Premier League football, and debates at the Parliament, and you'll be treated with dignity. Otherwise, you'll put pay your chances of any deal.

France

The French appreciate working with someone who speaks French. Meet your French counterparts for lunch or dinner and wine. The French tend to be the most relationship focused of the European countries, and meeting in person can help you pick up on cultural nuances you might otherwise have missed.

Russia

Don't expect a warm welcome in Russia. Large partners may discredit you and ask why they should be talking to you in the first place. This isn't because they're not interested; it's just their negotiation style adopted from the ex-Russian military in business. They are testing your ability to withstand the harsh business environment. A good tip is to find a level-headed partner to represent you in these talks. There are a lot of small Russian tech entrepreneurs who are scrappy and willing. Interestingly, with over 6,000 manufacturing outposts, German companies fare very well in Russia, so it may be wise to work a German angle.

In an interview with Nikolay Gulin, Russian market entry expert, he explained:

> Capitalism in Russia is still very young, and established companies dominate the market. New companies and entrepreneurs are looking for their niche to occupy an intermediate segment between large technology companies. While it's still early, it's also hypercompetitive.
>
> Relationships and reputation weigh heavily in people's minds in Russia. (This is the same in many emerging markets without a lot of governance.) Develop a broad network of people who want to work with you first. Without good business or personal contacts in the industry, you can rarely get the necessary decision makers. There is only a red carpet for you if you have something to offer that has a comparative advantage or a particular reputation through your network that has already been built up. Let me emphasize how important it is. When entering the market, you'll face many difficulties. Some of them can be solved after a simple phone call and the doors will open. Good networkers have a lot of different founder-level contacts who can help set up partnerships.
>
> Hiring local representatives in Russia is helpful. It's different from offer to offer and from product to product. Some are local advisors, government counsel, and others can be business development experts. Offer both a small salary and commission for reaching targets, but overweight the commission so they stay put and grow the business together. Business in Russia takes years, so don't expect fast results. As a reference, it took Nintendo nearly four years to set up the right partnerships.

SOME OTHER TIDBITS FROM ASIA

Japan

The Japanese hold formalities and cultural appreciation in high regard. They respect anyone who speaks a few greetings, bows politely, and understands even a bit of Japanese culture. Giving detailed answers and presentations is very much respected because it shows you put in effort respectfully. The Japanese take their time to vet any partners, so make sure you present well and note that they value team consensus in decision making. In traditional Japanese companies, it's very important to find and work with the decision maker. The CEO often is just a figurehead and relies on decision making from his executives. Breaking the hierarchy signals distrust and could ruin your relationship with the deal champion.

Much like the Germans, the Japanese are detailed and analytical, but they are also relationship driven. Gestures like small gifts or cards from home mean a lot. Due to new regulations after the financial crises, there isn't a big *nomikai* (drinking) culture anymore, but always remember, the Japanese respect those who persist. *Ganbarimashou!* Let's fight!

South Korea

South Korea is one of the trickiest places to do business. Although acting like a guest is expected in any country, this is particularly important in South Korea. Bringing gifts is appreciated, and showing deference is polite, but saying flattering and respectful things is the best way to win them over. It's also worth noting that South Korea falls between China and Japan in terms of style, pace, and culture. They tend to move fast like the Chinese but also follow formalities like the Japanese. Korean American Stephen Lee adds, "Like Japan, business decisions are top down, so it's critical to have engagement and support from not just the highest level but also middle management." And don't kid yourself: Koreans like a good time. I've visited Pusan and Seoul several times and have gone on food tours, hit in rooftop batting cages, ended up on a beach eating live squid, and drank my fair share of soju and beer—often together. Eating and drinking together is a strong part of their culture and considered to be where trust and personal relationships are built.

China

And last but certainly not least, China. China is the most competitive and regulated business market in the world. If you go there, go fast and take your best game. Once they sniff you out, it'll be a dog fight. Make sure you get the government's approval if you want a fighting chance. Another way into China is through Taiwan. Taiwan is technically recognized as a part of China, but because of the state's semiautonomy, businesses in the country have a long history working in the United States and Japan. They also have a more structured legal market and democracy. Setting up in Taiwan first is a path worth considering; it worked for me when I was the GM of Asia at Boku. On a side note, I've always found doing business in China to be fun and rewarding. The Chinese are fast, intense, and entrepreneurial; they live in the most competitive marketplace in the world. You can learn a lot from the Chinese business style; it's at least worth a trip, even if you don't set up shop.

India

I've worked in and out of India since 2003, when I worked in Hong Kong at a GE Asia Pacific Capital Technology Fund. Rather than give you my thoughts, I'll step aside and let Indian Silicon Valley entrepreneur, my ex-colleague at Boku, and Founder of Bureau Inc. Ranjan Reddy give his thoughts.

> Be ready for chaos. Although it's not a process-driven market/society, it's quickly evolving. Be patient, persistent, and have tact, especially when working with people across an organization. Often timelines won't be followed, so you must push people a little bit firmer and lay out clear instructions for what needs to be done. That said, even the maps may be thrown out, so be prepared with a plan B.
>
> Many Indians are relationship driven, looking for a long-term connection (personally and professionally). Make sure to

invest in relationships and not come across as transactional. People want to know you will be by their side over time. But what you see is not always what you'll get. Most people won't give you a clear no, so you need to always backchannel to higher-ups. That also means that you need to acknowledge the power of hierarchy and its importance in decision making. Without the boss's buy-in, any sale is difficult.

Vietnam: An Anecdote

Here is an interesting lesson from my travels, when I learned the power of getting the product in the customer's hands. I was riding a motorcycle through Vietnam and stopped at an ornamental mineral and tea shop outside of Hoi An. The salesclerk guided me to a seat and offered me tea. I sat down, relaxed, and held the mini jade teacup in my hand. I felt its warmth in my fingertips; I sighed, released my exhaustion. Pouring teacup after teacup, the salesclerk served me and let me gain back my spirits—somewhat caffeine induced. Thirty minutes passed. I had to get going and asked how much for the tea. He responded, "Of course the tea is free. There is no charge. But the jade teacup set is $300, and we can ship it to the USA. Wouldn't this be a great memory?" I was still holding the jade teacup; how could I not agree?

CHAPTER 12

HOW TO PRICE

"The three keys to pricing are familiarity, flexibility, and fairness."

—Nicholas Reidy, Silicon Valley Customer Success executive

Before you set out to sea, you and your team must determine how to price your product. This section is cowritten by Nicholas Reidy, who has served as a Customer Success (CS) leader for over a decade at several B2B SaaS startups (Boku, DocuSign, Contentful, and Fountain).

The price must be right. B2B SaaS startups' objectives are to acquire customers, grow top-line revenues, and increase profitability. Your pricing will vary over time with these objectives: the price to acquire a customer will differ from the price when "wringing the wet towel" and optimizing your deal. What it comes down to, however, is the right price and package to win the deal. Because without even winning the deal, the rest doesn't matter. No whammies. No whammies. No whammies.

What's the method for packaging and pricing? First, understand general pricing principles, then the models, and finally the tactics that will get the product in their hands.

1. General Pricing Principles

There are three general foundations for offering a price that won't surprise your customer: familiarity, predictable costs and ease of explanation, and fairness. You don't want them to close the door on you before you even get the conversation going. Like an architect, build a good foundation to start from.

FAMILIARITY: SELL SOMETHING THEY ALREADY KNOW

To avoid shams, customers buy products with terms they already understand. The less you need to explain your product and pricing, the faster
a customer can decide. Should your client already pay for Salesforce
on a per-seat basis, try to keep it roughly the same. There can be great
strategic reasons for choosing a new way to price your product, but you
must do so thoughtfully and intentionally.

Consider which department in your lighthouse account will be
making the purchasing decisions. If your target buyer is in sales operations, they will understand per-user pricing for tools that make the sales
team more productive. If your target buyer is in engineering, they may
be more familiar with consumption-based pricing (à la Amazon Web
Services). Anything that is not customary will cause headaches in the
customer acquisition stage, as companies will have to rethink their business model and legal terms to suit. Anything that is familiar sells fast.

PREDICTABLE AND EASY TO EXPLAIN

Create a predictable cost model that's easy to explain so that buyers
quickly ramp up. Buyers, especially finance departments, want to know
how much your product will cost as they roll it out. If your pricing
model involves many different functions, it's tricky for a company to
estimate how much they'll use each feature. Two risks emerge in this
situation:

- The first risk is that you might overestimate a buyer's needs and
  sell them too many units. In this situation, at best, it will be a
  long time before you get an upsell from that customer; at worst,
  your customer will be upset, demand to downsize their contract,
  and bad-mouth your company to others.

- The second risk is that you underestimate the buyer's needs
  and sell them too few units. Customers will get upset since
  they thought they had agreed to a specific price per month that
  meets all their needs, yet suddenly you're haggling for more
  money than the customer has budgeted.

Pricing should be predictable so that the buyers can run their models and easily calculate costs. Along those lines, it should be easy to explain and understand.

Transparent and defensible pricing models are critical. Clarity speeds up the sales process: the less time your sales team spends explaining how the pricing works, the more time they can spend on how great the product is, and the faster your deals will close. Defensible pricing also speeds up the sales process. Costs related to "how much the customer needs" are easy to defend; prices based on "how much money the customer has" are not. The last thing you want is for a new champion, buyer, or boss to cancel a contract because your pricing is confusing or seems exploitive. So keep it simple, stupid.

BE LOGICAL AND FAIR

Be fair, and don't milk your customer—or you're likely to lose them. In games of multiple negotiations, being fair keeps the game going; skinning the sheep ends the game.

An artificial limit is one way to anger your customer. It is a hard ceiling on something important, such as the number of users, that forces the customer to upgrade their whole plan to a higher-cost tier. For example, at the time of this writing in 2020, Salesforce's "Essentials" edition costs $25 per user per month but is only available for up to 10 users. If a customer wants an eleventh user, Salesforce forces the customer to upgrade to the next tier (the "Sales Professional" plan), which costs $75 per user per month. Essentially, the eleventh user effectively costs $6,900 per year. Some companies use artificial limits to achieve "price discrimination"— that is, charging people the amount you think they can pay. Artificial boundaries may work well for large companies like Salesforce, but most startups don't have that kind of market dominance and pricing power. Better not to even try that tactic until your market cap is $100 billion.

Another important rule is to set limits based on logic and estimation. Don't guess. For example, if your sales team has no idea how many API calls the customer needs, they will either undershoot, and the customer will have to pay overage fees, or they'll overshoot and sell

100,000 accounts, and the customer will feel "taken to the cleaners." In either instance, you've hosed yourself. If you can't estimate usage, don't pull it out of thin air. Start small and implement rolling pricing or tiered structure pricing. Start at a low volume and change the price as the volume goes up. That way, everyone has the same expectations as the account grows. Logic sets expectations.

Life isn't fair, but your business terms should be, roughly. Your customers will inevitably, at some point, compare notes about your contracts and pricing. Industry contacts talk to each other, and employees move companies all the time. When these conversations happen (and you may or may not find out when they do), you'd better hope your pricing is fair and consistent. Like the previous point about defensibility, the publication of prices based on customer needs won't cause blowback, but a customer paying more for the same thing will upset a peer.

A caveat is that early customers will have better pricing than later customers since they took a considerable risk on your company as a vendor. You should honor them for that risk and adjust pricing when and where it's necessary. That's fair, isn't it?

2. Pricing Models

There are three basic pricing models: percentage-based pricing, unit-based pricing, and a mix of the two. Once you choose a model, the next step is to consider how much incremental value to give per price and how expandable it is to your entire enterprise. Making the proper selection for your unit of value is the most critical pricing/packaging decision you'll make. Which units do your competitors and comparable companies use? Remember that familiarity sells: if all companies in your industry use the same unit of value, you shouldn't diverge from that unit unless you have a darn good reason.

PERCENTAGE-BASED PRICING

You may already have your model down pat, but let's review it quickly. Percentage-based pricing is frequently used for financial products related to transactions. If your product is transaction related (converting between currencies, processing payments, etc.), then percentage-based pricing is likely appropriate.

Another way to use percentage-based pricing is for shared upside—that is, risk and reward. A product that saves the customer money (perhaps by reducing travel costs) might have a price set as a percentage of savings. A product that increases revenues might have a price set as a percentage of revenue growth. This approach likely makes more sense for early customers when the gains aren't yet known or proven. Once the vendor has several customers, it will set prices in a more standard and intelligible way, but at the start, you'll need to do a bit of guesswork.

UNIT-BASED PRICING

Unit-based pricing is the second standard. If you go this route, your units need to be sensible and familiar, such as $X per widget, $Y per user, or $Z per usage hour. The unit can be based on the product itself, the number of people using the product, the amount of time spent using the product, or using any combination of those elements. "One of the keys to crafting a successful go-to-market strategy is to pick pricing and packaging that is scalable," says Jerry Chen of Greylock Partners. "A Unit of Value is the smallest measurable unit at which your product or service provides value."[14] The basis of this section comes from Chen's article on Greylock's website.

There are four primary dimensions: unit quantity, unit quality, unit size, and account features. A well-chosen group of values will help your business in two critical ways. First, you'll gain more revenue from larger customers while still offering lower price points to smaller customers. Second, if you have a land-and-expand model, you'll be able to earn more revenue from a given customer as their usage rises. Here are bundling tactics to promote maximum adoption.

Unit Quantity—Sell a customer more units of your product. Five sodas cost more than one. You are adding a numerical value to this. As mentioned above, the unit can be based on the product itself, the number of people using the product, the amount of time spent using the product, or any combination of those elements. One user, one server, one hour, and one API call all make sense. Be cautious and thoughtful about pricing based on the number of users. You want to promote the adoption of your product, and user-based pricing discourages experimentation and viral adoption. That means some products should be sold in bulk units, not by counting heads. If your product helps each user do his or her job better so that each user needs his or her account, then charging per user works.

Unit Size—Sell different sizes of your product. A large soda costs more than a medium drink. In software, size can be in terms of data, time, or seat usage. Jerry Chen gives these examples: teams (Box), entire departments (GitHub for engineers), terabytes of data (Hadoop), clusters of servers (Mesos), ERP for the whole company (SAP), and enterprise apps for the entire company (Oracle). Once you reach these levels, your CS teams need to be ready, as the customer will want to have the procurement and legal teams involved. In this case, one = many.

Unit Quality—Sell basic and deluxe versions of your product. Organic-ingredient soda costs more than the regular version. (You should be willing to sell both customers a mix of regular and organic pop; don't force an upgrade of all drinks to organic because they need one of them.) Email management software Mailchimp is a master at this. Project management software vendors like Asana do this well, too. They make it easy to adopt and more costly to add features. They also do a good job with multidimensional pricing, below.

Account Features—Single sign-on (SSO) likely only makes sense when it applies to the entire account. This feature applies to all the widgets and users in an account and should be part of an account-level upgrade. Some make the mistake of offering features as part of an à la carte update that can be mixed and matched with others. That lessens the profits. Another example is an uptime SLA. You'd better believe that a *Fortune* 500 company wants user controls for safety and data privacy. These types of features may include paying for controls and different access levels for different types of users.

MULTIDIMENSIONAL PRICING MODEL

Although it's not appropriate for all businesses, a multidimensional pricing model can be exceptionally productive and powerful for providing sophisticated customers with many ways to give you more money. Not every dimension will make sense for every product and business. In general, the more aspects you can use, the more flexible and powerful a pricing model you can develop.

A common concern is how to allocate different account features. Suppose you differentiate based on some combination of unit size, unit quality, and account features. In that case, you'll have to decide which features go into the "basic," "pro," and "ultimate" versions of your units and which features are attached to companies versus which features are on the account level.

Start by assessing which features only make sense to apply to the entire account. Security-related features (such as SSO) likely must apply to a full report, as will customer support levels. If, for example, a customer wants one department to use your high-security group and another department to have the low-security version, they should purchase two subscriptions with different feature levels. Team-enabling collaboration features are an excellent way to differentiate packages between hobbyist users and users' requirements at large corporations.

Once you've designated account-level features, assess whether the remaining elements are quality or size. A widget for which you guarantee 99.99 percent uptime is a "high-reliability" widget (a unit quality metric). In contrast, a widget that processes 10,000 transactions per hour is a "high-throughput" widget (more of a size metric). Dividing features between quality and size only makes sense if many of your customers need one but not the other. If that's not the case, bundling those characteristics together is a perfectly reasonable path. An example of this would be a high-performance widget that handles 10,000 transactions per hour and guarantees four nines of uptime. Bundle or split your widgets as it makes sense.

3. Pricing Strategy and Tactics

Now that you have some basic pricing guidelines and structure—or possibly one you are already using with the sales team—you are ready to think about your pricing strategy and tactics. It's likely you know your lighthouse account relatively well by now. What you don't want to do is slam something down their throat; instead, let them pick from a menu. Once they've chosen a plan, land the deal by delivering a high-value product and the price they want. Finally, expand to an entire enterprise-level contract. This pricing is the basis for your negotiations in Part 3: Land and Expand.

GIVE CUSTOMERS CHOICES

A happy customer is one who has been given several options. The unhappy one feels forced into spending more than expected because the only two choices offered were "not nearly enough" and "far too much." By providing a variety of options, your company will receive lots of smiley faced stickers ☺. Some businesses won't purchase if the only suitable pricing option is too sophisticated for their needs and too expensive for their budget. Add several other tiers so that you are in the ballpark of their usage and needs.

Beware: A pricing model that offers too many choices will also lose revenue. Some customers may be willing to pay the higher price for the "top-line" package because of one or two "must-have" features. A typical example of this is adding SSO capabilities: SaaS companies nearly always bundle the SSO feature with other higher-end "enterprise" features that sophisticated buyers require. Once again, keep it simple.

LAND THE DEAL BY PROVIDING FULL VALUE AT ALL DEAL SIZES

Let your customers fully experience the "meat" of your product; as mentioned, don't impose artificial limits. Your instinct might be to put the best parts of your product into the more expensive higher-tier options. This method often proves counterproductive since it blocks lower-paying customers from experiencing the total value of your product. Unable to find great use out of what you provide, customers will rarely upgrade or will end up dropping your product entirely.

I don't mean to suggest that you should only sell your product for a low price. Instead, structure your packaging and pricing so that lower-cost versions are constrained rather than crippled. Time-based or throughput-based limits are examples of how to do this. For instance, for $1,000, I can't buy a Ferrari, but I can rent one for a day and get all the thrills for a few hours. For a limited time only, they get the full experience.

In addition, requiring customers with sophisticated needs to make a large purchase will slow down deals, reduce your win rate, and make negotiations more difficult. Larger companies often have thresholds in their purchasing process; above a specific limit (e.g., $500,000), there will be additional signoffs and other requirements. Allow customers to get a foot in the door for a smaller amount. When deal size arises, the customer's legal team will apply more scrutiny and take a harder line about negotiating the terms. That means they'll take longer. The longer it takes, the more pressure your startup will feel to concede on a big deal when it may mean making or missing the quarter's revenue target—that's a common game the lighthouse will play.

PRICING TO LAND THE DEAL

How aggressively should you price? There is a bit of reverse psychology to it. You don't want to give too good a deal. Do that and the other side will be wondering why you are willing to give up the farm. They'll immediately doubt the quality of your product. Hold your pricing as much as possible and let them know your product will outperform. This is particularly effective when bidding against a few others. The competitors who immediately drop their price will be seen as more of a commodity. If you can argue compellingly that your product is better and worth the price, you'll win the deal. On the flip side, should your product be first to market and the lighthouse is the early adopter, you may need to give them a sweet deal—that is, whatever they want.

What that means is, you'll need to work on a few things to turn the deal into a moneymaker over time. You also can't break even or lose money in perpetuity. Calculate your marginal cost for the contract so you know you won't go out of business due to the concessions you made. Marginal costs include server costs, communication, rent and electricity, account management, engineering for customization, and even unexpected third-party costs. Once you know this, you know your walkaway, and if you can't walk away, at least you know how fast that customer will burn your capital so you can raise another venture round.

With that information, you can package your offer to get them on board. Here are a few ideas:

1. **Trial period**—Give them a free period with an unlimited cap on quantity; never put gates on adoption. You want them to use it, and under no circumstance do you want to limit that use. Give as much candy away as you can, and they'll buy after the free period is over. Subtly let them know how much it costs you.

2. **Bait and switch**—Sell premium but switch to the enterprise-level base version. Sell the all-inclusive version, but when they haggle on price, create a base version for them that doesn't include the premium features. Still sell them the Ferrari but without the premium features.

3. **Cost plus**—Know your walkaway cost and build off that based on your pricing model. If push comes to shove, quote them a cost-plus model for a capped unit quantity, while maintaining the quality.

4. **Risk sharing**—Do an initial performance-based deal where your company takes a risk. If your product increases their revenues or saves costs by X percent, then you get a share. If you outperform a benchmark, then that share increases.

5. **Up-front capital deal**—Create an up-front capital-esque deal structure where you pay up front for engineering, support, or marketing hours, then ratchet back the payments as revenues flow in. Keep your long-term pricing the same or even higher in the short term.

I always say, "Everyone wants a special deal." Your lighthouse account will want the most preferential one, but that doesn't mean you have to sell the farm. Discounts are acceptable, provided they commit to you. Here are a few that you can combine with the aforementioned packages:

1. **Exclusivity**—The longer the exclusive, the lower the price. The best way to put it is, "You commit to us, and we'll commit to you."

2. **Volume**—Of course, the more volume, thereby creating economies of scale, the lower the price.

3. **Service levels**—The higher the guaranteed uptime or the more customer success management time, the more expensive it is.

4. **Department level**—Sell it only to a specific department in an organization.

Let me elaborate on the last point. Be forewarned: Getting an enterprise license too early will often mean that you had to make substantial price concessions. How do you avoid that? Start with one or two departments, then expand to the enterprise. Don't sell the farm all at once. More on this in Chapter 18.

WHEN TO CUSTOMIZE

A special deal won't be the lighthouse's only request; they'll also require a special product. Customize your product if it helps you land it. Many executives argue that "customization is not scalable." They are right. It's not, and you aren't a unicorn if you think it is. That said, suppose you have your back against the wall and need to customize your product to win a lighthouse account. Do it, but set a limit and price on the engineering hours you're willing to offer. Charge them as much as you can for these hours. Hopefully, this customer is not unique, and they are the first of many. Get the lighthouse on board with custom features and then sell those features in an even more transformative deal.

Here's an example. At Boku, we had to customize several deals to learn how to integrate our technologies into new platforms. We often promised a level of up-front engineering or customization hours. One example of this was on smart TVs, another was on the Sony PlaySta-tion, and another was with Nokia's platform. When Microsoft bought Nokia, our relationship with Nokia made a deal with Microsoft more plausible. This customization work and the risks we took with Mic-rosoft then gave us our standout story for Apple. We were the only company in the cross-functional market on mobile, desktop, TV, and the other devices that Apple required. That was one of the key factors in winning the deal. Customizing a few deals helped us to develop the IP we needed to win bigger deals.

Ranjan Ready offers another perspective. Ranjan has started multi-ple companies where he worked with large clients to create a proof of concept. His team developed software that clients needed but did not charge his clients for hours spent designing it. In this way, his startup could retain the IP for the software. Ranjan also recently jump-started a new company through custom work with banks in the Southeast Asia region. His thoughts on doing custom work are below:

> Custom work is an ideal way to capture your first deal in a new market segment. The customer funds your business while help-ing you create product fit. After that, the product is replicable with similar customers. Customization particularly works well in nascent markets and in geographical regions where soft-ware development may be lacking, such as Southeast Asia apart from India.

Part 2 Review

Getting the crew ready to execute is the meat and potatoes of your plan. No BD Captain can sail solo. Once ready, create a plan and then maneu-ver your ship in a strategic advantage. Through either corporate devel-opment or international positioning, you can create distinct advantages that entice your lighthouse to shine your way. Then you want to control what you can control—how you maneuver the market and price your product. Messaging the market through PR and marketing can turn the light in your direction as a clear market leader and differentiated service. Then price your product to get it into the hands of your customers as easily as possible. This will help you keep a happy crew and land your ship, while feasting on the meat and potatoes and drinking martinis. Do all of this, and you've created a very clear path to…

LAND AND EXPAND

"The secret sauce—take it ashore!"

CHAPTER 13

THE DEAL CYCLE

"It's all about knowing exactly where the customer sat in the deal cycle and believing things would progress to the next stage. Constantly check in, keep pressure on them, and wait for the situation to change—always with a smile, of course. Never take things at face value."

—Maximilian Lehmann, SVP of Adyen and ex-VP of Boku

Part 3 is the secret sauce. All of the work to this point means nothing without landing and expanding the deal. This part, then, must be easy peasy, right? Wrong. This is where the line is drawn between the BD experts and the masters—the muscle behind the hustle. The ones who make the cut are the Navy SEALs of BD.

That sauce's main ingredient is the deal cycle or engagement flow of a complex sale. Not only is it one of the most critical aspects of your deal process, but it can also provide you with a sanity check. That's right: staying sane is part of the game. It helps you read between the lines so you can identify how the lighthouse feels and alleviate any concerns. The longer the deal takes, the more internal changes (technical or human resource) the lighthouse undergoes, and the more uncertainty that arises. The best captains can withstand the ebbs and flows.

The way to do this is to understand where you are in the deal cycle, which is defined by the five Cs of BD.

Engagement Flow

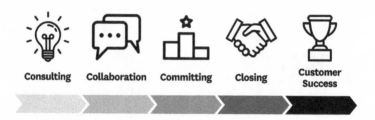

Consulting   Collaboration   Committing   Closing   Customer Success

Start as a consultant. A good consultant is liked, needed, and trusted. Your goal is to develop that rapport by showing them you are capable and committed to the relationship. Furthermore, you must have their best interests at heart, both professionally and maybe even personally. Show your contact not just the value of your product but also the value of the relationship. Engage them with case studies, recent news, research, and new developments. Be a thought leader for them. At this stage, you are going to give a lot more than you will get back, and that is what a good consultant does.

Mutually collaborate. At some point, the tide will turn and they'll start to reciprocate. That change indicates a good time to create a collaborative atmosphere. Hopefully, they will open up and share more information about their business needs and priorities. That's when the aha moments occur, and you can find product-market fit by connecting their priorities to your product. It takes two to tango.

Get them to commit. At this stage, it becomes a game of where you rank in their priorities and when they can commit to integrating. Once the large account realizes your value, add unique selling points to push your solution higher on their priority list. Make your product indispensable. The discussion is no longer about your value proposition; it's about the other company needing you. Finally, get them to commit either verbally or with resources to start the project. Hook them without a contract and get the product in their hands as easily as possible.

Close. Land the deal. This comes down to negotiations and contract terms. Frame your discussion points around building a lasting relationship that will improve the sustainability of both companies. To make your offering critical to their business, align your interests, resources, and efforts. Make sure you are going in the same direction together. This is when everything you said is now demonstrated in the contract. Put your money where your mouth is! But don't be cocky. During the negotiations, use empathy and reframing techniques to manage the discussion and emotions.

Customer success. Bust out the martinis? Not just yet. Now that they are on board, give them white-glove treatment and expand the account as far as you can. Customer success stands on three legs: project, relationship, and pricing management. Expand your contract to a multiyear deal. Do that well, and you can take a team vacation anywhere in the world you want and drink lots of martinis.

Noes and Yeses Mean the Same

At this juncture, I'd like to touch on how to read people's responses. I covered ghosting in Chapter 5. Some people won't ghost you; they will actually give you some type of answer. Ghosting, yes, and no really all mean the same thing, depending on how the other person communicates. Well, isn't that unexpected? A no isn't necessarily a no forever; a yes isn't necessarily "we are ready to go."

Don't take a no unless they tell you to "drop dead." Remember that noes aren't usually nevers. A no or "not now" may mean there is a problem with one of three things: you, the lighthouse, or the market. Let me go one step further. Take a no and replace it with a *not until*.

Not until…

1. your product gets better, your balance sheet firms up, or your price comes down (your problem);

2. our product roadmap lightens up, our internal organization restructures, or we have a deal leader (lighthouse account's problem); or

3. it's clear who the market leader is, the market isn't big enough yet, or the pandemic or some other geopolitical issue clears up (market's problem).

Keep digging until you get a clear definition of what a no or "not now" really means.

Depending on people's cultures, upbringing, and personality, you may often get a yes that means nothing more than "I certainly would like to speak to you again." In fact, you can replace the above *not until* with *yes, when* and it works almost perfectly. How bloody ironic is that? That's right. To qualify the yes, let them know you'll be sending a contract over and ask them to set a signing date. Then you will quickly find out what that yes really means. Keep these in mind during the deal cycle.

The Four Ps of Salesmanship

During the deal cycle, know how you want to be seen by the other side. You can't go wrong by remembering what I call the four Ps of salesmanship: persistence, patience, politeness, and pushiness.[15] You need to be all four, with varying levels of each. Early on, be more patient and polite; later, be pushier and a little less polite. Remembering these four attributes will pull you through the ups and downs of the deal cycle. Sure, there will be times when you want to say, "WTF?" or "F* this" or "Throw in the towel." But don't. Just keep at it and never lose your cool.

Sought-After Tips from a Former Apple Executive

Much of the special sauce I learned from James Higa, an ex-Apple executive who worked with Index Ventures at the time. Often, the best way to learn how to reach the land of lighthouse deals is to get tips from your network. Talk to your investors and tap veterans from large corporations on how they worked with startups. James's advice offers both a snapshot of what we've covered and input on what to do next. (Thanks, James.)

1. The initial discussion must have a significant global impact, demonstrating the ability to scale technology to millions of users with no hiccups. (Recall the section in Chapter 4, "Impact Wins.")

2. Give the lighthouse account all the support they require during the courting process. Deliver exceptional presentations and functional working demos. Do whatever they ask. Your support for them now will convey that you can withstand the pressure and execute up to their standards after the agreement (Chapter 14).

3. Care about the customer experience foremost. Make sure they know you care as much about it as they do. Do whatever customization or work required to show that you are aligned with them to find product fit (Chapter 15).

4. During the process, don't go above and beyond your deal partners; instead, stay steady. Don't force their hand by going over them, and don't let them force yours by threatening competing solutions—call them out. If they are moving forward, it will be evident by their communication with you. Let the current take you (Chapters 14 and 16).

5. Be aggressive on pricing, and make sure they know they are getting the best deal in the market, and yet don't be afraid to push back if they ask for *too* much. Also, this must be a low-risk investment for treasury and finance so that they will be drilling you on payment terms, exchange rates, payment timing, and more (Chapter 17).

Zen of BD

Before we jump into the blood, sweat, and tears of closing, I'd like to acknowledge that BD can be very stressful. In a survey by the online career database PayScale, sales ranked as the second most stressful job, with 73 percent of respondents rating it as "highly stressful." I've been there, and it is.

You know who doesn't get stressed out? A monk. But a monk doesn't make a good sales guy—if someone says no or nothing, he'll accept it and walk away. The monk thinks, "Let go of things not meant for you."

You are a BD Captain, not a monk, so you need to know when a no (or silence) is a "not sure" or a "maybe" and try again. By nature of longer sales cycles, BD executives will get more silences than sales guys will get. Those chirping crickets cause your anxiety to escalate. You react by checking your email every second lest you miss crucial feedback from the lighthouse. When you hear the crickets chirp, stay calm and rational. Busy, they must be.

Keeping this in mind, remember to take time for your own well-being as well as that of your team. I could write an entire chapter on this. In an interview with Ryan Paugh, salesman and life coach, he suggested the following:

1. Turn off all notifications. There is no room for mindfulness if your phone is deciding when and where your attention goes.

2. Before every meeting, check in with yourself. Do you know what points you want to get across? Are you emotionally and mentally ready? If not, what can you do to put yourself into a good mindset?

3. Take 10 minutes every day to train your mind's ability to focus. It may seem counterintuitive, but the more work I have, the more I meditate. It refreshes my mind and body.

4. Block time for deep focused work. Spend ample time working on presentations with your team, researching the market, and understanding your product better. Deep work is calming and will give you more confidence in the understanding of your product and internal business functions.

5. Stay levelheaded. Regardless of what happens, be emotionless. If you lose the deal and get fired, you won't be homeless. It's just a deal; it's just a startup.

CHAPTER 14

BE A TRUSTED CONSULTANT

"They like me, and they need me."

—Mark Britto

Now is the time to be laser focused on landing the lighthouse. You've gotten their attention. Now you need to demonstrate how you can help and build that requisite trust. Years ago, I consulted a former Andreessen Horowitz partner, Tim Dombrowski (also an investor in Boku), about selling to enterprises. He stressed four key points when working with lighthouse accounts:

1. Network up and down the company ladder, from the procurement people to the execs, searching for the deal champion. Anyone else involved in the decision-making process should know not just you but also other team members, scaling up to an investor or board member. The more people who trust you, the better.

2. Find a "friendly" who can help you to understand the internal status of the deal. This person will assuage the deal internally and sound the alarm if the deal is going off the tracks. Only friends trust, right?

3. Make them feel like it's their ideas and decision. Bestowing ownership is a key principle in any form of persuasion and leadership.

4. Do their homework for them; whatever slides or Excel sheets they need, lay it on a silver platter. They should be so comfortable that they treat you like a colleague—a subordinate, if you will—asking you to do whatever they need for them. If they rely on your work, they implicitly trust you.

Tim's advice is the gist of this section: develop relationships across the company, approach them with a consulting mindset, and add value with each follow-up.

Developing Relationships

To get your hooks into a lighthouse, network up and down the corporate ladder until you find a deal champion and a "friendly" who can give you the lowdown when things become uncertain.

FIND THE DEAL CHAMPION

Finding the right person to champion the project determines whether the sales cycle is reasonable or never ending. Do not underestimate the focus, persistence, and luck needed to get through to the right contacts in big organizations. It's a mentally and physically demanding process that requires constant attention to how you're navigating and communicating with your contacts at the other company. There's nothing worse than working with someone who claims they can close a deal and finding out six months later that they didn't have the power.

Figure Out Who Benefits the Most

The first question you want to ask yourself is, "Who benefits most from my technology?" This is different from "Who is buying my technology?" In fact, the user may be different than the buyer. Although it's important to know both, your initial contact should be with the one benefiting most from the technology. As an example, consider Stripe, the heavily loaded engineering startup. Since their solution was so much easier to integrate than other payment processors, they sold to engineers.

Engineers preferred to speak to engineers. The engineers who bought the technology would then flag the finance team to sign off on it. Sell first to the benefiter, and the buyer will fall in line.

How Do They Think?

Once you find the buyer, use your research to tailor your presentation and discussion to fit the way the leaders at your lighthouse think. It's easier than it sounds. For example, the odds are good that an ex-consultant will approach a business case with strategic reasoning. On the other hand, an ex-banker will look at numbers and ask questions based on high-level market analysis and financial modeling assumptions. A trained product manager will focus on customer experience, while a games payment manager will care about the best pricing model and someone with whom they can trade game tips. (Seriously, if someone works for a company that puts out fun or hot products, get to know them. Don't fake it till you make it; use the product.)

Are They a Mover and Shaker, Internally?

Knowing how they think will also help you understand their motivations. Each person's motivations vary at big companies. Some people want to secure their job and benefits with a nice bonus on top. These types respond by the fear of losing what they have. Others want to manage more people and grow their organization. Should your deal assist in that, it's a good sign. Before you get too deep with any contact, make sure you know their motivations and that they are aligned with you. The ones most aligned are likely to be the innovators and leaders with ambitions to get promoted within the company. They are the so-called intrapreneurs.

Tyler Epp, COO of Miami Grand Prix, agrees with that point.

The success of sports organizations, especially, is driven by the intrapreneurs within their structures; they are the ones that make an impact, being bold enough to make a hard business decision that has a direct impact to success, on and off the playing field. Find the intrapreneur—deal champion—who isn't afraid speak up and make a case, even when it is unpopular, and you will win.

That's the ideal champion—a mover or shaker who seeks change and gets along with others across the company. Most pipelines extend 12 months into the future, so find the contact who is willing to make your project one of their main ones for that time. They have as much risk in the game as you do. It's even worth asking, "What's your risk (upside/downside) if you do the deal, or if you don't?" Do a deal with them, make them look like an untouchable, and they will be by your side for the long haul.

Double-Check Their Influence

No doubt, there will be times when you question if your champion is really on your side. When this happens, approach the situation tactically. Ask your CEO or a board member to go in and find out what's happening. (That way, should anything go wrong, your champion can't come directly at you, and you can play stupid like you didn't know.) If they *do* find out and get upset, though, apologize and send flowers and chocolates. Be honest and direct. To avoid this happening at all, set up the tiering structure early.

If you are having trouble getting traction through your contacts, go top down: have the executives unlock a new deal. This approach was helpful when Boku worked with Spotify. Within a day of being introduced to the Spotify CEO, Ron Hirson and Mark Britto flew to Sweden to meet with Spotify. That meeting led to my introduction to Spotify's head of payments, and together we brought the deal home. That way, the CEOs had a relationship to catch up on the deal at any time. The operational teams executed the contract.

Be wary during this process, though. You never want to come across as overbearing, which can turn people off. In one such scenario, Boku made progress with a mid-level "deal champion" at a US carrier. A board member introduced us to the chief marketing officer (CMO), and we pushed for a meeting. Because we were just a startup, though, the CMO skewered us, telling us we had no viable impact on their business.

Remember that reorganization in companies happens. A lot. Even after you've found your champion, maintain other contacts at your target organization. If you receive that unwelcome email that says, "I'm no longer on your project," you'll have others with whom to circle back. You may get multiple emails like this throughout the deal-making process—I think we got more than two handfuls over a handful of years while working on the deal with Microsoft.

FIND A "FRIENDLY"

As mentioned in the introduction to this chapter, a "friendly" can help you navigate the deal with your partner. This person isn't on the deal team but is high enough in the organization to give you oversight and advice. Make the person part of your deal plan and invest time and resources in them, as they may be integral to the deal getting done. A friendly can also help block a new competitor, indicate where you rank in product priority, negotiate sticking points, and flag unforeseen road-blocks to the deal.

One example of how a friendly helped Boku was during the Sony deal. I met Joseph Tou, a leader in Sony's Corporate Development Department, at an Andreessen Horowitz showcase event. We connected immediately and became friends. He was instrumental in helping the two parties work together. Years after the deal, Joseph and I spoke about his involvement. He said,

> Overall, I think that the most important part I played was as an objective and neutral internal sponsor or champion. I paired up with the business unit executives—both in the US and EU—in charge, got to know different members of the Boku team, and then stood by Boku's side through the relationship. What that did was provide a level of comfort internally at Sony and cleared the path for a more trusting relationship. That trust resulted in a quicker and smoother business deal being done. I'm not saying the Sony/Boku execution was easy, but I would like to believe that we removed any obstacles, primarily those of questioning the gut or doubting the other parties' abilities and integrity, that can get in the way. We developed trust, on both sides of the table.

The Consulting Mindset

Begin with the consulting mindset, or they'll show you the door. The consulting mindset starts by offering more information than you get back. You are just here to help, often shooting in the dark, throwing out ideas. When they start asking or pulling more information out of you is when you know you've done it well. Let's get the conversation started.

GETTING THE CONVERSATION STARTED

I touched on this idea in Chapter 5, but let me elaborate more. Always start first. This sets the tone that you're the commander of the deal. At the beginning of each meeting, show the other party the agenda you've prepared, and then let them decide if they'd like to follow it or be more casual. By beginning this way, you signal that although you're the one in charge, this isn't a one-way street. If you make a hard sell, you'll never get the dialogue you need to succeed.

So get them talking. Once the conversation has started, keep inviting them to talk insofar as they'd like.

- "Let me know if I'm talking too much. I really would like to get to know about your interests." *Some presenters ask for questions at the end, but this isn't a press conference, so let them ask during the pitch.*

- "I bet our companies are similar in that…" *At this point, you want to start connecting with the other person and drawing parallels to company working style, similar goals, and cultures.*

- "You seem like a rational and knowledgeable person about this space, and I don't want to tell you information you already know. So tell me, what are your interests or requirements so that we can understand your objectives?" *Labeling the other person in positive terms will perk up their ears and let them like you more.*

- "Tell me more about…" *Keep the other side speaking as much as possible.*

THE YES CONSULTING MINDSET

At this point, you can do anything, so answer most of the questions with a "Yes, and…" Your goal in the conversation is to uncover the other party's current challenges and priorities. During this process, you may discover that they need something your company doesn't currently have.

Many times at Boku, lighthouse accounts asked if we could offer a certain service, technology, or support. Even if we didn't, our answer was always, "Yes, and…

- Here are some additional ideas on top of that we can do as well." *Treat it like a great idea and add more ideas on top of it.*

- "We'd be happy to expedite it if you're on board. If you can commit to us, we can commit, as much, to you." *Demonstrate that it may take effort to deliver what they want, but you are happy to do the work should they commit to you.*

- "We need to understand the problem you're trying to solve a bit better, then confirm it with our technical team to get it on the roadmap. Shall we set up a meeting with our teams to discuss?"

- "We need to understand your technical specifications to understand how it would fit with our current product." *The last two scenarios are a great lead-in to fast follow-up meetings with the technical teams. The quicker you go deeper by connecting teams and talking technology, the stronger the hook.*

Generally, saying "no" or "I don't know" is a losing position. If you really can't or don't want to do it, then be truthful and let them know where you stand. Sometimes a hard no engenders trust in the dialogue. But if you really want to work with them, then just qualify your yes. Beware of selling the farm or having to backpedal later by not qualifying your yes.

What if you just don't know the answer? Then try these to duck and dodge the conversation:

- "I don't want to misspeak, so I'll get back to you in 24 hours."

- "I don't know, but my CTO does. Let me get back to you."

- "That's confidential information. We haven't signed an NDA and don't have approval to disclose that information just yet."

- "We haven't looked into that yet, but let's talk again soon and walk through your idea." *Turn it into an opportunity to meet again.*

Once you've finished your discussion, end it on a good note. Here are some lines I use when closing a meeting:

- "Out of respect for your time, let me know if you'd like to keep pushing forward or if we need to pick this back up later."

- "We really appreciate all of your ideas, so please give us some time to digest them and send back how we can accommodate your needs." *Praise their ideas, even if they were yours.*

- "I'm honored that we've made it this far and hope we can continue." *I like to use the word "honor." In Japan, it's standard and names the mutual respect necessary for most successful meetings.*

- "What concerns should we address when we follow up? What's an appropriate next step that we can both agree on?" *Get them to agree, or you'll be throwing darts back at them.*

- "Before I leave, I just want to remind you of our two or three key differentiators and work with you on those." *Always remind them what you want them to remember. They are busy people, too!*

- "It's been great getting to know you. Even if we aren't a fit, we can learn from and help each other." *Acknowledging that the deal may not fit eases the pressure and lets the other party know that the connections formed will benefit you both. You may be surprised when they respond, "We absolutely want to keep working on this.*

DISPUTE MISCONCEIVED NOTIONS AND TOP-OF-THE-MIND PROBLEMS

One of the previous questions, "What do you know about us?" will reveal where you stand vis-à-vis your competitors and what gossip has been spread. Don't be afraid to dig even more by asking such questions as "Where did you hear this?" or "What else have you heard?"

Quickly identify any misunderstandings your lighthouse may have. Whatever it is, nip it in the bud. Reframe their thoughts. "You may think ___, but there's a bit more nuance to our work than what you're saying." Maybe they assumed something about you based on hearsay. They don't know your strengths because you haven't released them to the public. "You might think that, but let me tell you our perspective, how we do it, or how that's just wrong." As soon as possible, identify any thinking errors you can pinpoint and work to change those perspectives.

Of course, do all of this with tact. You don't want to offend customers by telling them they are wrong and coming across as a know-it-all. Take the indirect approach; start sentences with qualifiers like "In our experience…" and "We've learned…" When you disagree with your prospect, don't tell them straight up but illustrate your view with an anecdote of a customer success story. I've said before, "We've considered this, but it hasn't been a significant demand for other clients; here's why…" Be indirect and understanding. Your goal is to get them to see you as someone they can work with over time, so be tactful.

If you can have an open dialogue like this, you are on the right path. Keep digging to make sure they lay out all their concerns on the table. In doing so, you can quickly uncover *their* problems—the problems you can help solve. If you can't identify any problems and show them you're their solution, you're not making progress. Consultants can only succeed with a free flow of information.

An example of this was Apple. Apple thought that carrier billing was only necessary for Korea and Japan, where mobile carrier payments were long established. I knew our payment system was accessible globally, though, and I needed to show them this. In our follow-up meeting, we were prepared with an Excel sheet showing the dozens of countries where our payments system could work using macro- and microeconomic data. They were impressed and convinced that our solution could solve their global needs. We went on to fight another day.

Add Value to Follow-ups

Each follow-up should add value to the conversation. Essentially, you are giving them ideas to enhance their business—and their careers. Keep the dialogue warm, and call your friends when you need some help.

HOT TO ADD VALUE

Follow up with information your prospect needs to make a case for your company internally and set the next meeting. Sneak in your advantages and repeat them over and over. It will take multiple interactions before they buy in wholeheartedly. Consider these questions:

1. Do they need more market research?

2. Do they fully understand your capabilities or need more in-depth product flows?

3. Did they voice a concern that you haven't answered?

4. Did they seem hesitant, or did they tip off interest in a competitor?

Keep up the cadence of information exchange. Send your prospect announcements, either about your company or where the market is heading. Or you might want to send research you've found that they may find helpful (append the email with "No response needed"). Keep a list of bullet points from the meeting, and remind them what a good idea they had—even if it was yours. By doing this, you communicate that you are partners who add value to each other through sharing information and helping each other out. Make them feel supported in any way possible by a steady flow of information.

The king of building telecom relationships, Kevin Grant, shares some great advice and phrasing to advance business relationships. Here are a few of my favorites:

- "Not sure if you know this, but here is an inside scoop..." *Kevin doesn't reveal confidential information but just shares info or knowledge about the industry.*

- "I recently learned a few nuggets about some changes in the industry and thought they might be helpful to you." *Give free information up front, and don't ask for anything in return. It's like building a little credit. Give now, and they will give back later. (This is also the principle of reciprocity by Cialdini.[16])*

- "How can this deal help you personally?" *This question can reveal a lot of information. Once you become integral to a person's job, then you are essential in their life. They will consistently rely on you to get a step up or be the hero within their organization.*

- Whatever you do, try to add value to the relationship with each follow-up email or call. You want them to think, "Kevin always has something for me."

KEEP THE DIALOGUE WARM

Big companies get busy, reorganize, and then forget about or lose small discussions in their pipelines. It's your job to keep the heat on. Sometimes they unintentionally ghost you. And then again, sometimes they do it on purpose. Perhaps you are getting beat by a competitor. Perhaps you are behind a key market trend that the lighthouse wants and they don't have the heart to tell you. Perhaps internal discussions are taking longer than planned. Lesser companies often give up if the lighthouse doesn't follow up with them. Don't be one of them. Always keep the heat on using these three methods.

Do Their Homework for Them

That's right. Do whatever work they need so you aren't waiting months for them to create internal documentation. Don't be shy; ask them, "Shall I make this for you?" or "Why don't we send over what we have, and you can use it as you need?"

At Boku, we followed Kevin's advice from the start of a partnership. We passed legal, in-depth market and regulatory analysis to compare notes and assumptions. We built financial models that allowed our partners to plug in their premises and model out scenarios. We carefully wrote out presentations they could copy and paste into their company template and present internally. As they prepared to issue an RFP, we sent them a list of so-called sample questions for the RFP. If they needed talking points about our competitive advantages, we laid them out. In essence, we become part of their team.

Be in the Neighborhood

When you get ghosted, don't take it personally. Instead, reestablish contact by creating an opportunity for an impromptu, in-person meeting. Let your connection know you'll be in the neighborhood and would love to swing by. You may be around for another appointment (which is probably another cup of coffee, decaf, please), or it may just be a way to get them to respond. Either way, you're more likely to get a response with an "in the neighborhood" text than yet another follow-up email. (And if they *still* don't respond, then you might just show up at the office with a gift or card. "Even if you don't love us, I still love you." I've done it all. It works.)

Max Lehmann, whom we talked to in the international section, had used the "I'm in town" tactic many times—sometimes even when he wasn't. In one case, he sent an email to a client on Monday saying he'd be in town the next day. To his surprise, they said, "Let's meet Tuesday." The client was in the United Kingdom, so he flew from Germany overnight. In another situation at Boku, after two years of working on a relationship with Netflix, Max was ready to write off the opportunity. Before he did, though, he decided to send a haphazard email saying he'd be in town in San Francisco soon. (He was in Singapore.) Surprisingly, Netflix replied and said they would be interested in meeting later that week. Max jumped on a plane the next day and catapulted the deal forward. If he hadn't sent that one last email, Boku's deal with Netflix might never have happened.

Do BD for Them

Another way to keep your lighthouse account engaged is to do BD for them. As you get to know their business intimately, you can introduce them to your contacts, send them internal research, or even help them with investor introductions through your venture capitalists. Venture capitalists have clout and appeal, so introducing your lighthouse account may help them in various ways. Show them that you're interested in becoming not only a long-term partner but also a committed friend. Essentially, you are giving them a pillar of support, helping them in their career by building their network, whether now or later.

DON'T TAKE OUR WORD FOR IT

At some point, you'll get sick of talking or they will get sick of hearing from you. So let others do the talking for you. There is no better way to build trust than to get others to validate your sales points. Getting your existing customers to sell your product for you is one of the most potent moves there is. That said, in BD, there's a catch: a lighthouse account may not care about early adopter references. Early adopters may not have the same use case, technology requirements, and commitments that your lighthouse needs. A lighthouse wants to know that they are working with the most competent provider out there. For this reason, the most recent references ice the deal.

Without Facebook's help, Boku would have gone bankrupt. Our co-founder, Ron, led a charmed offensive to onboard Facebook. He also spoke to their existing social game customers who operated on the Facebook platform. Among them, Playfish/EA and a few others (some of whom weren't even our customers at the time) supported our cause. These social game merchants wanted to optimize their revenues and, to do that, needed an option with more global coverage. Boku was that option. Getting stakeholders or customers of the lighthouse to vouch for you can set you apart from your competitor.

Later, after partnering with Facebook, that relationship also helped us land a deal with Apple. Apple wanted confirmation we were indeed the best in the market. We needed to put their fears to rest, so what did we do? We got references from Facebook, Sony, and a few other customers of course. They vouched for our ability to execute new technology requests quickly, and voilà, Apple was convinced.

CHAPTER 15

COLLABORATE–PRODUCT FIT AND PRIORITY

"Figure out the job that your customer hires you to do. That may be unclear at the beginning, but the more you dig, the more it will reveal itself."

–Jon Prideaux

Figuring out the precise job that the customer hires you to do—that is, product fit—is the essence of BD. The key sought-after outcome of collaboration is twofold: mutual product fit and high prioritization. To achieve these goals with your lighthouse, you must first nurture a very collaborative and trusting environment.

Boku Founder Ron Hirson has a video on YouTube called StartupBD3: Ron Hirson Keynote. He describes salient BD tactics, but Ron's secret power was how he created a collegial atmosphere and strong relationships with lighthouse accounts by working side by side with their employees. Becoming a trusted confidant to your partner is key to exchanging information and figuring out how to work together.

The goal of the tight-knit collaboration is to find product fit that's acceptable to both parties and prioritize the product. It's tricky to do when large companies have a product roadmap planned years ahead.

Here's how: be part of their team, find product fit, and increase your standing in their internal roadmap.

Be Part of Their Team

You want to be an inextricable part of your partner's team, not just someone passing in the night. In the last chapter, I mentioned doing their homework and doing BD for them. That's just the start. Gelling with your partner often requires dozens of in-person (or Zoom) meetings—sitting in the same room, whiteboarding it out. You must share information, both negative and positive, with your partner so that you always know where the deal stands. Be honest about your weaknesses. An open and transparent relationship allows both parties to find product fit.

You also need to consider timing. Make it clear that you're serious about getting the deal done. Ask questions like "How would you like to work together?" or "What works for you and your company policies?" Or ask, "How would you feel if we got a few more engineers and product guys in the room?" These questions will help set the table for executing the deal. (It's always good to get the product team and engineers working together on technical co-development.)

In other words, don't just feel things out. Get in the same room and talk it out. At Boku, we flew our engineers all over to sit at client sites and read well-documented APIs. Absurdly, we would even travel to read publicly available words off a screen to members of the target account to make sure that we answered their questions correctly. We traded technical specifications documents to know exactly how the products would integrate and what adjustments to make. We both wanted to make sure the partnership would work, so we left no stone unturned. Be part of their team decisions as much as possible. Your expense account may suffer in the short term, but you'll get paid back handsomely in the long run.

Find Product Fit

Again, Jon Prideaux stresses this facet: "Figure out the job that your customer has hired you to do. That may be unclear at the beginning, but the more you dig, the more it will reveal itself." Sometimes you have to just keep digging. At Boku, our partners hired us to acquire new paying users. In turn, when we discovered this, our attention turned to user acquisition cost and lifetime value.

This benefit was not apparent with Boku's traditional early adopters. The early adopters used the technology to "make more money" through customers' impulse purchases. Later, larger companies used our technology to bring customers into the system who didn't have credit cards or other payments on file. That was our hook for acquiring new customers and keeping them for long periods.

How did we learn this? As we acquired more accounts, we learned more: Sony, Facebook, and others demonstrated that we were in the business of acquiring first-time buyers—people who paid for the first time. That's what Apple wanted. Back then, Apple needed a way for iPhone users who didn't have credit cards on file to buy their services (this was particularly common with customers in Asia and Eastern Europe). Our pool of funds at the carrier was the perfect solution. The product they needed was a payment method that could be on file and cover consumers in these markets. Once we figured that out, our product team worked incessantly to deliver it. Thus, by using our product, Apple was better able to accomplish its strategic mission of earning profit from software services.

Adapting product to make it fit lighthouse account

PLAY YOUR CARDS

You've spent time and money building out your competitive advantages and gaining market share—these are your aces, kings, and queens. You may have a product with competitive advantages far ahead of your foes. By now, your geographic presence may stretch wide and far; hopefully, you have customer traction that others could only wish. Which advantages does the lighthouse value the most?

Your Aces Up Your Sleeve

Features, Scalability, International, Customer Success, Market Leadership Position

Play them one by one until you win. What I mean by this is play to your strengths in terms of product, competitive advantages, and team abilities. Their eyes will light up when you play the right one; then you know what card could win the deal.

Every card won't win of course. Customers won't always receive your product fit ideas with open arms; you must continue moving forward to show your partner you are engaged and resilient. Everyone makes mistakes, and if you suggest and miss, don't worry. You most likely have multiple hands.

How did we learn this? One such example was when our BD team was meeting with Apple's technical team. Now that our company had a bigger vision that competed with other payment forms like gift/prepaid cards, we had to deal with more obstacles. Apple's head of gift cards was not overly excited to work with us because he thought it would detract from his business. We assured him that wouldn't be the case.

After the meetings, one of our team members, Welly Sculley, devised selling prepaid Apple gift cards via carriers. It was a great idea, and although it didn't pan out in the end, it *did* help to win over the head of gift cards who felt threatened. Apple politely declined and asked for a different use case for a one-tap checkout flow. Over the next month, our product teams worked together to make it work.

The significance of this story is that we kept the conversations going, alleviated a key team member's concern, and waited for the right time to push our main selling points. (It's usually best to wait for the other party to discover their need rather than for you to peddle it to them.) It just so happened that we had already executed a similar product and were on time for their new request.

Adapting product to make it fit lighthouse account

GET THEM TO FLIP THEIR CARDS

This isn't a poker match, so don't be afraid to ask your lighthouse account how you compare and what other projects they're working on. You want to know as much as you can about where you rank against the competition and the internal product queue. You want them to flip as many cards as possible so you can play the right ones. (Figuring out how to head off the competition comes in the next chapter.)

So you've spent a lot of time creating spreadsheets and analyzing the market. What makes you think that they aren't doing the same? You bet they are. Here is a spreadsheet used as a priority scorecard from a large technology company. Just remember, you are just a score, too.

Corporate Scorecard

Project Number	1	
Project Title	Project "Navigate to the Lighthouse"	
Total Score	**895**	
Deal Type	Payments	
		Score
Partnership Benefits	New Internal Capability	20
Partnership Benefits	Establish Industry Standards	10
Partnership Benefits	Reduce Costs	20
Partnership Benefits	Access New Technology	20
Partnership Benefits	Address Competitors	30
Partnership Benefits	Enter New Market(s) or Market Segment(s)	20
Partnership Benefits	New GTM or Sales Channel	20
Partnership Benefits	New Revenue Steam or Monetization Model	20
Strategic Fit	Optimizing Internal Technology	20
Strategic Fit	New UX or UI design	20
Strategic Fit	Internet of Things	0
Strategic Fit	End-to-End Security	20
Strategic Fit	Control the Endpoint	0
Strategic Fit	Gives User Controls	20
Executive Sponsorship Level	General Manager Level	150
Opportunity Size	$500 MM - < $1 BN	150
Time to Opportunity Realization	2-3 Years Out	80
Gross Margin Profile	Enhancing > Existing	100
Competitive Intensity/ Differentiation	In Line with BU	50
Partner Attractiveness	Medium Partner (Top 5 in Project Market)	37.5
Alliance Track Record	No Alliance Track Record	37.5
Risk: Technical, Development, IP, etc.	High	0
GTM Risk	Medium	50

This scorecard is a snapshot of what could be on the list. Here are some common big company criteria when evaluating partnerships:

- Executive sponsorship is a big driver ranking from C-level, general managers of business units, and product managers. Without one of them, it's tough to get in the queue.

- Partnerships should be executable in a reasonable timeframe aligned with the roadmap of the company. Something that isn't a high priority stretching out over three years will be disregarded. A high-priority problem that your technology can solve will leap the queue.

- Align with existing strategic pillars for the corporate. It's easier for the puzzle to fit. If your technology is so new and has yet to be evaluated by a corporate, it will take up to a year for this evaluation.

- Look at gross margin accretive. Most corporates evaluate partnerships on a gross margin basis for that business unit.

- Projects need to result in 1 + 1 = 3 when looking at revenues, customer expansion, geographic expansion, competitive positioning, and so forth. (I discussed synergies in Chapter 8.)

- Identify the strength of each potential partner. Enterprise software companies would rather do deals with other equally sized enterprise companies, not a startup, all things being equal. At the very least, the startup must be well funded and have the wherewithal to sustain. Involving a new partner in the ecosystem takes a lot of heavy lifting internally, so that company better have the resources and staying power.

- Look at market leadership. If the category is in a startup space, then they want to see clear market leadership. (I addressed how to do this in Chapter 10.)

Once you've got a feel for how you are being assessed and for your spot in the queue, your next goal is obvious: climb the ladder. To do this, you'll need to learn your partner's business needs, even if they are unrelated to your own. Certain partnership benefits will be evaluated more highly than others. Find those and go one step further; get them to reveal their key performance indicators (KPIs) or yearly goals. Knowing this can then help you adjust your product or make a new business case. Do this as early as possible—after all, although time may not be an issue for your lighthouse, it is for you.

Are they most worried about performance, price, scale, or ___? Ask them.

- "I don't want to push you but just wanted to get an idea on how the process is going. Do you see any roadblocks?"
- "What are your most crucial decision points?"
- "How would you rank us in terms of priority and how we rank with the most critical decision variables?"
- If you can't figure out where you stand in the queue, remember your "friendly" and ask for advice on the internal workings of the company.

When working with Apple, it wasn't until we asked them about their international priorities that they told us. We thought we were helping them bring down the fees to save costs on other payment forms, but they were more concerned about their consumers who had no payment attached to their iTunes accounts. By having a phone number that could act as a credit card, they would convert more users over time. We needed a seamless product that could fit into their billing platform, coverage of markets (about a dozen in Asia), and fees roughly aligned with their other alternative payment forms. When we realized this, our strategy changed to focus on other markets rather than worrying about pricing.

Pricing was not their priority, so after we expanded throughout Asia, our place in their queue skyrocketed.

KNOW WHEN THE TIDES TURN YOUR WAY

You know you've leapfrogged the pack once the lighthouse starts to ask for more information. Being the lead dog by no means guarantees you'll close the deal, but it *does* mean that you're able to drive the conversation at the pace you require.

Here were some indicators at Boku that the tides had turned our way. Several times, companies asked us for sample RFPs. Others would make strange requests such as "Can we see your balance sheet?" or "Could our boards meet?" Listen for subtler signs as well. An executive once told us, "Your team is very creative. That's exactly the kind of partner we want." Generally, companies like to work with other companies on par with themselves.

CHAPTER 16

GET COMMITMENT

"I am out here for you; you don't know what it's like to be me out here for you. It's an up-at-dawn, pride-swallowing siege that I will never tell you about. Okay?! God. Help me. Help me! Help me, Rod. Help me help you..." says Jerry Maguire to his troublesome client, Rod Tidwell.

Rod replies, "I'm sorry. You are hanging on by a very thin thread. And I dig that about you! No contract? I'll help me, I'll help you, help everybody? That's my man."

Jerry: "Hey, I'm happy to entertain you."

"Help me, help me!" Rod mocks him.

Frustrated, Jerry turns on his heel. "See you in Los Angeles."

"Jerry, c'mon, man. That's the difference between us—you think we're fighting, and now I think we're finally talking."

This dialogue is from the movie *Jerry Maguire*[17] and is the type of business power struggle you'll experience at some point in your BD journey—constantly fighting for the deal. It will not be a friendly, cordial relationship all the time. To have a bit of a tug-of-war, you must develop a healthy relationship from the get-go. You want your lighthouse account to know you're trying to do right by them; they need to understand that a deal gone awry will hurt you both—the risk isn't one way.

When Jerry Maguire walks away from Rod in the middle of their conversation, he indicates that he can't take it anymore and isn't sure the effort he's putting in to close the deal is worth it. As a result, Rod chases after him and changes his tone. Sometimes that's how you're going to have to act to get the deal you want. Maybe you should do the same: let the lighthouse know that you, too, will walk away.

Rod is now ready to commit to Jerry, and so is the lighthouse for you. They must stop shining their light for other boats and focus only on you. You've rolled out the red carpet, materially invested in the relationship, and developed a collaborative product fit. Now you need to get them to see you as an equal. How do you get them to do this? Turn the tables and get them to commit.

To turn the tables your way, you must get the lighthouse moving toward a decision, fend off the competition, even the playing field, and get a verbal commitment. Do this successfully, and the rest is just paperwork.

Getting the Lighthouse to Dance

Lighthouses move notoriously slow because of their internal pipelines and processes. They also realign departments frequently, so it will behoove you to get through as quickly as possible. Sometimes you may have to sell a competitive fear to pick up the pace. Or sell that the hands of time are ticking. Maybe they just need to be aware that you, too, can walk away. Sometimes you have to toughen up.

In the first case, let them know that time is no longer on their side. As a BD Captain, you need to get deals across the finish line, and this one is taking too long. Try these:

- "We're putting a lot of time into this deal, and I need to be sure that it isn't wasted. Can we put a date on this?"

- "I'm getting a lot of pressure from my CEO to bring these discussions to a conclusion. I'm sure you understand. Maybe the CEOs should meet to push this to a final date?"

- "Off the record, what's your point of view on the likelihood and timeline of closing this deal? If this deal doesn't have legs, it'll be my head and bad for our entire company, especially after investing so much time."

- "If we can't commit to a date, at least let me know that we are your preferred choice so I can keep spending time."

James Higa mentioned you shouldn't make threats but that sometimes you may have to indicate there are other options if your partner isn't moving fast enough. Here are some phrases you can use to nudge them along:

- "We only have time and resources to work with one large partner, so we need to get a commitment soon or we'll have to turn to elsewhere."

- "We are talking with your competitor and they're moving faster. They see this as a potential competitive advantage over you." *If this isn't working, then push harder…*

- "We are doing an exclusive deal with your competitor for a limited time. We need to get the show on the road. So unless you're ready to move, we will go another direction." *A friend of mine once used this on a payments deal; it was untrue, but it worked.*

It's tough to draw the right line in the sand. You need leverage; otherwise, you're making soft threats that will come back to haunt you. If you do make a threat, make sure it is credible and that the other party is in the position to answer it. Otherwise, they'll counter by inviting in new competitors. Below is how to fend them off.

Beat Back the Competition

Remember that cannon back in Chapter 4? Pull it back out! A lighthouse account will have multiple suitors. If you don't have any competitors, congratulations to you; feel free to skip this section. What you don't want is for them to ghost you because they are leaning toward a competitor. Or even worse, get a phone call at 5:00 p.m. on Friday that they went with another vendor. There are a few tried-and-true ways to figure this out. The key points to remember are don't be a mind reader, pull out the cannon when you need to, try to call a face-off, and if all else fails, drop the Hail Mary bombs.

Reading minds is vexing, so here are a few lines to help you avoid this:

- "Let us know if you are considering other options and how we can counter them. We'd like to know where we stand at any time."

- "We'd love to know what you've heard about us in the market and why you may be reluctant to work with us. At least give us a chance to dispel these notions. If anything, it will make our business better, too."

- "Please give us the opportunity to make a final proposal before making any decisions. We want to put our best foot forward." *There is nothing worse than being blindsided by a customer you've been speaking to for over a year.*

- "I haven't heard back from you in a while. Has the situation changed, or did something happen internally?" *Let them say no and backpedal or yes and provide a reason.*

- "We've been working together for a while, and you also seemed concerned about the chances of this deal. Is that so?" This is a labeling technique, allowing them to open up. In *Never Split the Difference*, Chris Voss says, "Labeling is a way of validating someone's emotion by acknowledging it."[18]

Sometimes you'll need to pull out the cannon to fight off the competition. Pull out that cannon again and add some new cannonballs.

Here are a few more ways to sabotage your competition:

Use logical reasoning to explain why you've chosen your course and not the competitor's. Perhaps the said advantage is merely a feature that can be replicated, or perhaps it's not as important as what your company has chosen to do.

- "Sure, our competitors may tell you that X is an advantage, but we chose not to do X because we thought Y and Z were more critical for success. We also feel Y and Z align better with your interests."

- "Like you, our resources are limited, so we try to invest in what makes sense for the most significant opportunities. We haven't invested in the features you think are attractive because…"

Evoke doubt by casting objections or calling into question the veracity of your competitor's accusations.

- "I suggest you double-check that they can do what they say they can. Some of our other clients have experienced otherwise."

- "If it helps, we will contractually commit to addressing your doubts. Will they put on paper what they pitch?" (More about this in Chapter 17.)

Use math to beat them with the sum of advantages or the wash method.

- "Our competitive advantages are X, Y, and Z. If you look at the math, our company will net you more money/benefit you more." *Sum of advantages.*

- "Our companies both offer features X, Y, and Z. So that's a wash. But they offer A, and we offer B. B is more valuable than A." *That's the wash method.*

Once you've created an inkling of doubt, call a face-off! In the case that you are trying to overtake a vendor that already works with the company, your goal is to get them to let you run a head-to-head race.

- "Is your executive team comfortable knowing you committed to one partner for such a critical part of your business? Wouldn't it make sense to have an alternative provider to have a backup or redundancy? Why not have a face-off?" *This works when there are many options in the market and the customer has chosen to exclusively work with one when working with two or three may give them more bargaining power.*

- "If we and your current provider are competing for your business, we will have to compete in pricing, too, and will ultimately lower your costs." *Then follow with...*

- "We aren't afraid to compete with them. We've beaten them in X, Y, and Z accounts. Just give us the chance and we'll prove it. We can start with a small portion of the business, prove ourselves, and then expand." *This was one of my favorites.*

If you feel that you have, in fact, lost the deal, or you're just late to the game, then you may need to drop a few bombs.

Here are a few phrases:

- "If you don't give me a shot, it may cost me my job (or the business may fail). That may not matter to you, but there is a lot of pressure on me to get this deal done." *This is a desperate statement, but if it is your last chance, then it doesn't hurt to be honest. It also lets them know how important this deal is for your company internally.*

- "We've spent a lot of time working together on this, and it's ethically wrong not to continue. You even said we'd work together, and now you are going against your word." *Guilt trips work.*

- "This decision is against anti-competitive laws and isn't fair. We can take legal action." *This complaint was the go-to tactic for the CEO of one of our competitors when we started to get traction against them. Threatening to sue your customer sounds illogical, right? Strangely, it brought buyers to their knees—even though we all know in Silicon Valley there is no such thing as antitrust. That said, it's a particularly valid assertion if the company didn't issue an RFP.*

- "Let me be totally frank with you: you are making a bad decision. You'll regret your decision over time and will end up switching to us in the long run. Let me save you the grief and embarrassment of telling your boss you need to switch later. Here's why…" *Don't call the other person stupid, but let them know it's a really bad, illogical decision that will come back to haunt them.*

Even the Playing Field

Up until now, you've likely rolled out the red carpet for this account and beaten back the competition. Assuming you didn't lose the deal, let's even the playing field. Mike Ghaffary, former VP of BD at Yelp, now venture capitalist at Canvas Ventures, says you should treat large accounts like the best thing in the world and make sure they know they are getting the best deal, product, and service imaginable. That said, once your prospect commits to you, don't be afraid to ask for things in return. After all, the deal needs to benefit you, too. They wouldn't want to bankrupt your company, would they? That wouldn't make any sense. Roll out the red carpet, but don't give them all the crown jewels.

One way to do this is to make yourself look like an equal power player and, in doing so, get a verbal commitment from the large account. One of my old colleagues in China, Jeff Wu, was a master at this. He would approach big companies like Baidu and Tencent, and by pushing them and making our company look like an equal power player, he'd pull out a verbal commitment.

He was also very good at getting large accounts to move. How? He leveled up to them. He'd say things like:

- "We are the global market leader in payments; we only work with the best and biggest companies. That's why we're choosing you." *They looked bemused. Running through their minds was, "Someone is choosing me?" Not the other way around. But he made it clear: even though he was the lesser company between the two, he was the best in the business that they needed. Powerful tactic.*

- "We know you are a fast-moving company; we are, too. We've already prioritized it. Can you commit to a date on your roadmap so we can work together to a launch? If not, let me know so I can pull back the horses." *He implied that our startup was just as capable and already committed. If they weren't equally committed, he'd back off.*

- "I'm spending time on this because I think it makes a lot of sense. My time is valuable as well, so please be respectful of that." *He knew how to turn the power tables.*

BE IN THE BALLPARK WITH PRICING

At some point in the discussion (perhaps as early as the first few meetings), the lighthouse will ask about pricing. Usually, they want to know you are in their ballpark as they don't want to spend a lot of time talking if pricing isn't. Initially, the response I used was, "Let's talk pricing once you know this is the product you want." If they are harping about pricing, then they may only be buying on cost. You want to steer the conversation to your superior product capabilities.

That said, they may push back and say they don't want to waste time if you are just too expensive. That's reasonable. The cardinal rule is to delimit a price range so that you don't fall out of their boundaries. Ways to ask this include:

- "How much of a priority is price for you in your decision variables? Why don't you tell us? What kind of deal range and budget would work for you?"

- "Our price depends on other factors of course, including usage, exclusivity, time, and so on, so we'd have to get further into that first."

- "Let's be up front, we won't be the lowest cost provider. Is this okay for you?"

- "Once we provide a quote, can we have an honest discussion where it falls in your expectations and compares with others?"

Get Verbal Commitments

Once you've agreed on the price range, you're in the driver's seat. Getting a green light now gets you incredible leverage. Some say you are your word, and many people live by this. I've seen corporate-level executives invest in companies because they promised the entrepreneur they would and didn't have the guts to back out, even when the deal didn't look promising after due diligence. *How absurd!*

Create mutual commitment. Tell them you're invested in them and committed to the project. Make your own risks and interests crystal clear. Often, a big buyer will think they are taking on all the risk and giving you an opportunity. Let them know and then invite them to commit back to you. That acceptance will even the equation.

Here are some lines I recommend:

- "We will both be successful if we make this deal work. This is something we've tirelessly worked on, so let's get it done. Do you agree?" *Make it personal between you and your partner. Forget about the companies and how much money they'll make out of the deal. Make it something unifying and enduring between the two of you, something to tell your grandkids about.*

- "We've shown that we want to work with you, so can I get a commitment from you that we are your partner of choice? I need you to shoot straight with me so I can get our ducks in a row internally to service the deal." *Everyone wants to be a straight shooter.*

- "We need to get moving on your product development. If I can commit to getting you exactly what you want, such as the release of this feature by X date, would you commit to pushing to get the deal signed by Y?" *Duck trade to get commitment.*

- "We've found product fit and we've agreed on pricing. What more do we need? Let's go ahead and commit to this and get it on paper with the lawyers' oversight." *Take it out of your partner's hands and put it in the lawyers' hands.*

- "How are we going to celebrate once we sign off?" *Be presumptive. You'd be surprised what vacations people spout out.*

DON'T CLOSE PAST THE SALE

Motormouths don't close. Once a customer has agreed to work with you, shut down the sales pitch and talk about hobbies, movies, or sports, not more about the deal. Make it seem that it was matter of fact. *We did it and it's done.* Some salespeople continue to discuss the value proposition, repeat points, and even talk about ancillary ideas. In some cases, I've seen salespeople talk themselves out of or invite competition into a deal. When you get a commitment, thank them, end the meeting, and let them know you will send them a contract. Getting a contract in the customer's hands not only helps get the legal process started, but it also keeps you at the top of the priority queue.

In one example, I visited a customer at a conference. By habit, I always brought a few contracts in my briefcase to leave behind. While at the meeting, the CEO said, "Let's do this." I smiled and said, "Sure. Shall we sign on the dotted line?" He agreed, and with a few swipes of the pen, it was done. It didn't make our lawyer very happy, but the deal performed well.

A Verbal Commitment by Sony

Boku had been working on the Sony deal for about six months, and we were now meeting weekly in London. In these meetings, we discussed technical specifications, legal concerns, financial payment issues, and more. We knew there were competitors aggressively knocking on the door because Sony was constantly mentioning them. We knew we needed to get Sony to commit as soon as possible.

Once we had addressed the outstanding technical issues, we discussed deal terms to be sure we were on the same page. The market rate for our service was known, but Sony was a big client and wanted the best terms. We needed them of course, but we couldn't handle operating at a loss. By all means, though, we were going to give them what they wanted.

The Managing Director of Europe invited me into his room to talk about pricing. He wanted to make sure we both had the "same pricing expectations." He led with a price that undercut the market by half and a request for most-favored-nation (MFN) status. It was a good flag in the sand from his standpoint. I was a bit caught off guard. (In the next chapter, I discuss more about putting a flag in the sand.)

An MFN for Sony would shake down our already tiny profit margins. He refused to give us an estimate on how much volume would go through our payment channel. I told him he was getting the best deal in the market at that moment in time. Going forward, we couldn't predict the future, but we could revisit over time as volume increased. With the advice of our GM of Europe, James Patmore, we swapped out the MFN and a no-volume commitment with a touch of a higher rate. We shook on it with the caveat that I had to get the CEO's approval. (They still needed to do an RFP per company guidelines, but we were clearly the leader.) Over time, our terms with Sony changed for different countries and services, but what was important was to get the commitment and get our competitors locked out.

CHAPTER 17

CLOSING TIME

"It's okay to spend time arguing about which route to take to San Francisco when everyone wants to end up there, but a lot of time gets wasted in such arguments if one person wants to go to San Francisco and another secretly wants to go to San Diego."

—Steve Jobs[19]

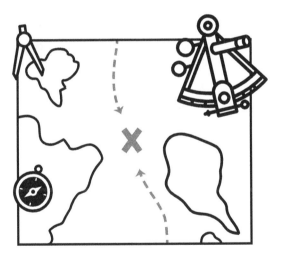

Negotiation is often where the ship sinks. Too often, people go into a negotiation assuming they'll have the resolve to get a good deal. It often doesn't happen. The single biggest piece of advice I can give is to go into the negotiation with the mindset that this partnership is a team and must work for both parties. The next biggest is to focus on the issues/problems and not the person. Do that, and you'll sail through any strong winds.

Before you can address any roadblocks to the deal, you must make sure you and your lighthouse account are both heading for the same objectives. Lay out mutual goals, be transparent, and engender trust. If one side is being deceptive, you may not both end up at the same place. That trust you've built until now should be the foundation for the negotiation.

There are many books written about negotiation. I'll cover just a few items that will help the ship get docked at the lighthouse.

Here they are: work together like colleagues, study the tricks of the trade, put your flag in the sand, show empathy, and reframe.

Working Together like Colleagues

I said it once, twice, now thrice. First, create a collegial atmosphere and say something like "We are working together. We want you to succeed, and you want us to succeed, so we need to make sure this works for both of us." Set this atmosphere up front. By doing this, you knock down barriers, alleviate anxieties, and create collegiality.

To create this environment, you may need to reveal more than you think you should. In one case, I asked a partner to trade Excel sheets to understand what we were missing. I first learned this trick at a Duke MBA negotiations class and employed it during my time working with mobile phone carriers. For rational people, this method works well. Once your partner understands your cost of servicing your business and profit margins, they are more likely to consent to your needs. By following this advice, Boku did this during the Apple deal and nearly doubled the initial deal price they offered. This tactic works especially well when your back is against the wall.

EXECUTION PLAYBOOK

One of the best ways to build trust with your client and create a collegial environment is to write up a post-deal execution playbook. This playbook lays out not only the tactical execution but also how you fore-see the partnership evolving. This document details everything from post deal handoff, step by step integration, test rollout, full rollout, and post 12-month expansion plans. Let the other side provide their $.02, and they will feel that you they have clarity and control that the exe-cution will be successful. At Boku, we did this with all of our major partnerships.

Tricks of the Trade

There are a few tricks of the trade that are worth listing in order of action. These are imperative to make the discussion go swimmingly. Let's lay them out.

The first one is to lay out all the variables when starting the discus-sion. Do this because it will impact how you correlate and trade vari-ables. You don't want to agree on a variable and then later go back and renegotiate it.

Know what's most important to you and to them. If you are faking what's most important to you, then it may be difficult to rectify it. (Do you secretly want to go to San Diego?) Whenever possible, be clear about what's most important to you. (There is one caveat to this. Some-times the other side will assume something is important to you that actually isn't. In this case, use that assumption to trade off for something that *is* important to you.)

Make correlations clear. Often, variables are related to each other. Price is not a stand-alone variable. If they want more use, high guaran-teed uptime, or several account members, the price changes. Make sure that you clearly explain these correlations.

Draw boundaries. Let the other party know when they've gone too far.

Separate legal and business variables. Often, these can be negotiated separately, so don't be afraid to say, "Let's hash out the business terms and let our legal departments cross the t's."

Give early. Be the one who makes concessions early. That will start the dialogue and make your partner feel at ease. Remember, reciprocity.

Take breaks if you need to. Negotiations can be complicated and strenuous. When they are in abeyance, walk away. It's okay to take a few days off and reset if necessary. During these breaks, don't think about the deal. Take time off completely.

Know when to walk away. You don't want to land a lighthouse in a broken ship with no resources to expand. Have clear lines in the sand. Your partner will respect you for this. You, too, need to make money to support them and be the best possible partner. It's worth noting that most big companies have a lot of money and pricing isn't usually their main concern.

The Flag in the Sand

There are many viewpoints on how and at what price to start a negotiation. Some say you should make an offer that nearly makes the other party walk away. Others say to avoid making the first offer entirely. Although this second tactic sounds good in theory, it's quite hard to do. A door-to-door salesman isn't going to ask, "How much are you willing to pay for my product?" Instead, he'll state that he will sell you X for Y amount. Custom has made it that the seller puts the first offer.

In addition, unless this is your first deal, clients already buy your service at some rate—there will always be a precedent to follow—and most large customers will want a discount. These two factors prevent any significant unpredictability in the negotiation.

Here is what I have learned. Before sending a proposal, start a dialogue. I cannot stress how important it is to set expectations and discuss the negotiation before putting it on paper. Ask pointed questions to gain information.

- "Before we get into the details, I need to know what deal structure will work best for you." This statement usually gets a response like, "Keep it simple and like something we've done before." *That's the importance of Chapter 12.*

- "What do you think your potential scale or usage amount will be?" *Get this information to help with volume pricing.*

- "How do you feel about pricing? What's going to work for your budget?"

- *Pushing even further, you can throw out a range.* "I think we're both thinking in this range. Am I right?"

- *If you feel your back is against the wall:* "You want us to make money and succeed, don't you? You want us to be happy, right? Clearly, you wouldn't want your partner to go out of business."

Notice that all of these are setting expectations that you aren't going to let them run over you. It also begins the dialogue. That's a big victory and the critical first step to get people to work together well. The next step is to transpose your sales pitch into the agreement: put your money where your mouth was.

Put Your Money Where Your Mouth Is

You've promised a lot until now, so the best way to close the deal is to put your money where your mouth is: commit to future products or pricing. That's where you'll win real trust. When sending a contract, translate all the competitive advantages you claimed during negotiations into action. If you told the lighthouse account you have the best uptime, put that in SLA. If you committed to providing new features within a certain amount of time, make that happen and throw a penalty on yourself into the contract if it doesn't. In other words, use the initial contract to show your commitment to your word.

Here are some good examples:

- Contractually guarantee to execute a product within a specific date, and if you fail, pay a fine.

- Even better, commit to a future price or volume-based pricing based on a change in the market—trigger pricing. If this happens, you automatically get a discount.

- Guarantee revenue generation over an existing competitor if you want the lighthouse account to switch to you.

- In your SLA, commit to a performance or feature set that no other can match.

These are ways to win the deal without negotiating only the price. I've done all of these methods successfully, so give them a try.

A last point is that if you need to invest in your own deal, do so. Through co-marketing and advertising, and integration and development costs, you can show your lighthouse account just how committed you are to the deal. This can also pay off by giving you greater leverage to negotiate a higher recurring component of the deal. You can tell them, "By investing up front, we want to lock in a rate over time." If you are confident about how your product will perform, this tactic can increase long-term revenues.

Here is an example of putting your money where your mouth is. Once while working for Boku, I pitched to a small games company that had integrated our main competitor. The buyer was very sharp and rational, yet fair and opportunistic. I told them a story that we'd outperform them due to X, Y, and Z features. He believed me but couldn't justify the implementation unless I was at least two times better. We committed to a guaranteed uplift of 167 percent, or else we'd pay the difference. We won the deal and reached 210 percent on our uplift.

THE NEGOTIATION: EMPATHY AND REFRAME

Jessica Notini, professional mediator, trainer, negotiation coach, and facilitator practicing and teaching in California, divides negotiation into

three functions: process or setting the ground rules, relationship building, and the negotiation/transaction. Too often, negotiators jump into
a negotiation without any type of guardrails. The process of establishing boundaries helps you learn how to work smoothly together. Relationship building creates a friendly working environment and develops
trust, and the transaction knuckles down on difficult discussions and
substantive deal terms. Before you get into the heat, talk about how you
are going to talk about it.

Set Ground Rules

Setting ground rules for the negotiation process is critical. Ground
rules prevent things from getting rocky, thus creating a cordial atmosphere. If everyone follows established guidelines, it's easier to sort
out differences. Before you start your negotiation, discuss what these
ground rules will be. That's what I like to say: talk about how you
want to negotiate. In this way, both sides will follow them. Here are
a few ideas:

- Be respectful and collaborative.
- Disagree without being disagreeable.
- Speak softly.
- Critique and offer suggestions rather than criticize.
- Be concise.
- Stay on schedule.
- Focus on goals.
- Do not interrupt.
- Allow everyone to participate equally in discussions.

Foster an Understanding Relationship

The next part is relationship building. The best negotiators listen and
observe. Listening builds rapport and will give you access to more information. To listen well, give your complete attention to the other party.
Once they've shared their perspective, repeat back to them what you're

hearing them say about each point. Doing this helps you reinforce and check the accuracy about what you've heard from them. Last, if you're not sure about something, ask them to clarify. Understanding the other party is key to building a lasting relationship.

Once you feel you understand their perspective, show empathy. Sympathy is agreeing or aligning yourself with the other party; empathy is putting yourself in their shoes, not necessarily aligning/agreeing with them. As a negotiator, you are a mediator and must advocate for not only your own interests but also those of the other parties involved. Mediators are careful to remain neutral but empathetic to both parties. If you as the mediator do this correctly, the other party will be more likely listen to your ideas when it's problem-solving time. It's a subtle technique, so here are some sentence starters:

- "In your view…"
- "In your experience…"
- "I can feel you are hurt…"
- "It sounds like…"
- "I hear you saying…"
- "I'm sensing…"
- "That sounds hard…"

Done well, empathy can open doors and create a free flow of information. Finding out the other party's problem allows you to set the terms during the negotiation. This is what you want! Replete with information, you can knuckle down on the negotiation process and start crafting solutions.

Control Your Emotions during the Negotiation

During the negotiation, it's important to focus on a mutually beneficial purpose and learn to reframe. These two skills will control your emotional responses. "We want to help you improve so we can both improve." To establish and maintain this mentality, keep these points in mind:

- Be curious and humble.

- Focus on problem solving and learning from the other party, not punishment.

- Focus on mutually defined goals.

- Don't make important decisions on the spot.

- Don't talk about someone's character. Instead, discuss intent versus impact versus intention versus character.

- Seek the other party's meaning and perception or interpretation rather than claiming one "truth." (But don't ignore verifiable data.)

- Discuss contributions to problems rather than looking for fault and someone to blame.

Problems will inevitably arise in some negotiations. Someone may be pushy, which can lead to polarization. Solving problems without enough information can lead to an impasse or a series of suboptimal solutions. Overgeneralizing a situation may upset the balance of power between the parties. What's worse than the problem, however, are negative reactions to the problem. Resistance, anger, and indifference have no place in negotiations.

For this reason, if tempers ever begin to flare, take a moment to check yourself. Instincts in tense moments tend to evoke a fight-or-flight response. You don't want that. Instead, remember the bigger picture and where you want to go. Consider the other party's perspective, including any cultural differences you may have.

Once you're calm, address the other person with an "I" statement. "I feel...when...because..." and "I would like..." Don't accuse the other party of wrongdoing. Just tell them what you're thinking and feeling. When you do this, keep it simple and diplomatic.

One of the keys to overcoming problems is to edit or "reframe" a negative statement made by another negotiator into a positive or less damaging statement. Repeat their words back to them in the way you *wish* they had said it. To help yourself with this process, ask yourself questions like:

- What's the need behind their complaint?
- What are they afraid of?
- What is the purpose of these questions?

In other words, don't run away from complaints. Instead, learn from them and use them to guide your conversations.

An example of this: If they say, "These delays are outrageous! You can't run a business like this. We'll go elsewhere if this continues."

Your reframe: "It seems this delay has had a serious impact on your business, and better schedule adherence is important for you to want to continue doing business together. Let's work on that together."

Another example: "You took over the negotiation and made unilateral decisions every step of the way."

Your reframe: "So you really wanted to be consulted and involved in all decision making, and you are upset because you feel we did not allow for that. Let's go back over the variables and discuss one by one."

Or they say: "I won't accept less than $10,000 for this contract, and your offer of $5,000 is insulting."

Your reframe: "It sounds like you believe the contract is worth significantly more and our offer is not in the ballpark. Let me understand your reasoning more."

It's about Relationships

Something I learned in Silicon Valley and Asia is that a contract is just an agreement to start a relationship. Regardless of what the terms say, terms can be renegotiated at any time. This also includes your employment contracts. The value you may bring to your employer on day one will undoubtedly be different than what you bring two or three years down the line.

For this reason, don't stress if you end up with terms less favorable than you want. So long as the contract won't bankrupt your company, it'll work. It's better to prove your worth and satisfy your partner because once you're executing and doing great work, you'll be in a better position to renegotiate for mutual benefit. That's the job of your CS team who'll step up to secure the longevity of the deal.

CHAPTER 18

CUSTOMER SUCCESS– EXPAND THE DEAL

"Like startup investments, most BD deals fail. So choose your partner wisely and remember that signing the deal is just like raising venture money: it's a good start, but most of the work is yet to come."

–Matt Eggers, investor at Breakthrough Energy Ventures

You've landed the deal; now sit back and count the money as it rolls in. Hold your horses! It ain't over until it's over—don't bust out the martinis until the deal is live and profitable—that is, expand it.

Once you've won your lighthouse deal, execute on your promises. Your lighthouse account is your first referral in the new market, and their success determines yours. If the deal fails, so does your future. Because of this, your CS managers need to work hand in hand with the BD team to bring home the bacon.

When a company's pricing model, GTM motion, and CS models work together harmoniously, customers are happier and revenue goes up substantially. Giving prospects a smooth "on-ramp" allows them to learn about the value your product brings without forcing them to make a major purchasing decision. This on-ramp reduces the risk for buyers, which in turn speeds up the purchasing process. Customers who feel they're treated well—and more importantly, treated fairly—during this process are far more willing to increase their spending with you over time. For this reason, it is critical that the BD and CS teams operate like clockwork.

There are four parts to the CS process: the handoffs, project management, relationship management, and pricing management.

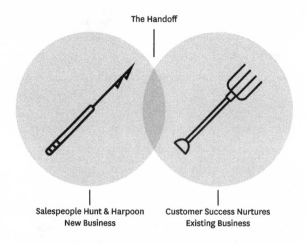

The Handoff

Salespeople Hunt & Harpoon   Customer Success Nurtures
New Business   Existing Business

The Handoffs

Passing the customer baton is very much like a relay race. Instead of three, there are two exchanges that need to be executed flawlessly. The first handoff occurs from BD to the CS integration manager. The second is from the integration manager to the CS manager. How should that work? My friend Nicholas Reidy says, "It depends."

There are several ways that a handoff from BD to the CS implementation team could work. One way is that once a contract is signed, the business developer/salesperson should step aside (though it's okay to keep an eye on things and track progress). Sending a friendly "Hello" email never hurts, but this person should not attend tactical onboarding or implementation meetings. This is because the salesperson will have built a good relationship with the customer by now, so the customer will naturally orient themselves toward the salesperson. Also, as the vendor, we want the implementation team to be able to operate autonomously and effectively without the presence of the salesperson.

There are a few problems with this method, however. First, the salesperson has built a close relationship with the customer: there is a lot of trust involved in a deal and that trust isn't developed overnight. Next, the salesperson may negotiate an adverse deal, taking the biggest bite of the apple up front. Because of this, it's likely that many deals will be oversold. Doing so puts the entire relationship on unequal footing, relying on the CS manager to balance things out and scramble to justify the high price. The relationship is set up to fail.

How do you prevent this? There are two models that make more sense in a modern land-and-expand context. The first is a lightweight relationship management function. In this scenario, for example, the salesperson intermittently checks in at quarterly business review meetings. The CS team leads the meetings and the agenda, but the salesperson is there as a form of continuity. Some models extend this relationship over years. That model may make sense when the expansion of the deal lasts for a long time. This is rare, however.

Another model is the upsell model. The salesperson remains attached to the account and has the right to all the upsell opportunities in a given time period—usually one or two years at most. In this way, the salesperson won't oversell the client and will reap the rewards for the long sales cycle. In either case, it's best to cap the time the salesperson is involved. At least 75 percent of the time "hunters" need to find new lighthouses to land, while the "farmers" should nurture the account. Even in the upsell model, limit the time of the salesperson's involvement post-deal.

Next, the best way to ensure this is to have a two-step CS process: the implementation team and a relationship team—the second handoff. Take note: Account growth should be organic and allow the customer to expand at its own pace.

The CS organization has an implementation/adoption team and a relationship team. The tactical lead should be somebody on the implementation team. The tactical lead's responsibility is to take the new customer from the implementation cycle to full adoption. It's a critical function for usage growth. At that point, the second handoff occurs—this time, to the ongoing relationship management team. The head of this team may be referred to as a CS manager (formerly called an account manager). This person has the ongoing relationship, commercial, and contractual responsibilities—in other words, they make sure the relationship is going well and the deal is profitably growing. If you pass the baton effortlessly, your customer will see how in sync your company is and trust you with even more business.

Project Management

So what does customer success management (CSM) do? High-level CSM teams coach clients through a project's execution. This starts when the BD lead hands off the large account to the CS team, or more precisely, the integration manager. This should happen during the later stage of the collaboration process when the dust has begun to settle on the deal. You don't want to wait too long because your partner needs to know who their long-term contact will be, and your BD person will soon need to head back out to sea.

UNDERSTAND ROLES

Finishing a handoff in a timely fashion is always challenging, so it's important that everyone understands and executes their role in the process. The CS manager's job is to use the business plan from BD to organize the internal team. By acting as a funnel and the middleman, the CS manager can keep priorities in check and move things along efficiently.

BE ORGANIZED

There is an old saying, "Overdress your client." Along these lines, over-manage your client by staying organized. Use whatever software tools you can to ensure your process is tight. Create a client onboarding checklist including introductions, agendas, briefs, and progress reports. Setting expectations and executing against a timeline is the single most important job in project management. A customer confident in your abilities to work with them will reward handsomely.

DON'T STRETCH YOURSELF TOO THIN

CS managers often manage many accounts, but a lighthouse deal may require more than one manager. Take this into consideration when you negotiate pricing. Charge more for each dedicated CS you add to the team, and don't worry that your buyer won't agree. When Nick was at DocuSign, one customer paid $20,000 per month for two CS managers to manage their account—dedicated account managers give the buyer an insurance policy. A big buyer doesn't want the deal to fail and will happily pay for the help they think they need to succeed, especially if they are paying in the millions for the software.

Relationship Management

In an interview with Silicon Valley CS executive Joanne Liu, she said, "The art of customer success management with prominent companies comes down to awareness, organization, and responsiveness—oh, and don't forget to just be human."

Being aware is critical to relationship management—the human or emotional element of the partnership. If key contacts in companies have different personalities or don't get along, the relationship will fail. For this reason, it's important to pair complementary people together. If your client is pushy or high maintenance, pair them with someone who can handle a strong personality. Conversely, some people are quiet and may need a more aggressive counterpart. Find the right match, and don't be afraid to switch account managers if things aren't going well. Turn your awareness dial up when it comes to managing the relationships.

Grasp the cadence of communication and how responsive the customer wants you to be. Figure out their communication patterns and needs. Create a contact schedule and measure how often you contact them every month. Let your client tell you when too much is too much. It's far better to be over the top than to undermanage your client because if you undermanage, you're more likely to lose your partner to a more attentive competitor. Many clients are okay with a response time of two or three days, but some may want to hear back sooner.

Deliberate communication underpins the relationship. Remember, "The customer is always right." Not. This relationship is a partnership, and by this point, you should feel comfortable telling your lighthouse account (very politely) when they *aren't* right. They don't know the ins and outs of your product. In these situations, first praise and thank your partner for taking the risk with you and *then* point out your difference in opinion. The happier and more appreciated your partner feels, the more open they'll be to listening to what you have to say. So be sensitive and deliberate.

Treat them like they're your best friend because in the business world, they are. Your best friend would want you to be aware, responsive, and sensitive—wouldn't they?

Pricing Management

I spoke ad nauseam about pricing in Chapter 12, so I'll be brief. There are four scenarios in pricing management: the deal is profitable and the customer is happy (good); the deal is unprofitable and the customer is happy (bad); the deal is profitable and the customer is unhappy (bad); or the business model is changing, and pricing needs to be changed (neutral). Regardless of the circumstances, your goal is to expand to a multiyear, enterprise-wide deal. Let's work it.

TURNING AN UNPROFITABLE DEAL INTO A PROFITABLE ONE

An unprofitable deal is better than no deal, so at times the BD team may inadvertently structure a deal in the red. Or maybe they just erred. One of the main goals of the CS team is to give your company more leverage and steer any deal into the black. The first and most natural step to getting leverage after closing is to make them happy. Yes, make them so happy that they'll be unlikely to switch to a different company when you come back to the table. Kindly remind them that you, too, need to be a happy vendor.

Once they are delighted with the features you sold them, then create boundaries to protect yourself, and insist that they pay more for added features. In doing so, they may ask for development help that isn't in the contract; gently point them back to what they agreed to. If they continue making these requests, you may need to suggest going back to the drawing board so that they're getting the service they need and you're getting compensated fairly. After all, they don't want you to go bankrupt—especially once they figure out that they really, really need you. Set your boundaries early and always smile when they cringe.

A PROFITABLE DEAL BUT AN UNHAPPY CUSTOMER

On the flip side, your BD team may have padded their bonus by negotiating an unfavorable deal for your customer. A classic example of this is when the customer buys more of a product than they'll be able to use during the initial purchase term. With an oversell, the CS team is in emergency mode from the start, scrambling to get a high enough adoption that a massive downgrade or cancellation doesn't happen when renewal time comes around. Because of this, never knowingly and willingly exploit your client.

If this ever *does* happen, give back to your customer before they are aware of what happened. Lower your price; throw in some bells and whistles—do whatever it takes to even the playing field. Even a small token will make them happy and build trust.

CHANGING PRICING OVER TIME

Do your best to "measure twice, cut once." You should make significant changes, like changing your unit of value, as rarely as possible. Considerable pricing changes disrupt your company: sales, customer success, marketing, product, and finance will all be affected. Customers and prospects who understand the old pricing model will need help understanding the new one.

That said, the market changes, and you will need to adjust. You can make small adjustments to list prices (but not the overall model) up to two times per year without difficulty. If you make changes more frequently than that, you'll have a hard time keeping your sales team updated on the latest figures, and new prospects may feel unfairly squeezed.

Few pricing models will survive even the next three years unchanged. You'll change your prices, learn from the market's reaction, and adjust. Be prepared for those changes and make it clear that your prices are not static, especially when it comes to new features. Build a "services offering" in your base product that allows you to charge different customers different prices for the same product, or a slight variation of it. A product's price will not be uniform. Be clear with this up front and over time as you roll out new features and services.

A/B Testing Pricing

A/B testing price is not advised in an enterprise sale setting. A/B testing is essentially an experiment where two or more variants of a page are shown to users at random to determine which variation performs better. While A/B testing is excellent for testing website changes, it's not a great tool for testing price changes. If your price points are relatively high, it will be hard to have a large enough sample size to show the effect clearly. Many other factors come into play, such as the skill of the sales rep, or the customer's industry and size, among others. If your price points are relatively low, then your customers may find out that you're offering different prices to different buyers, and you could easily have a PR mess on your hands. It's better to have time-series testing—for example, raise your rates 10 percent for a month for all customers and see what happens—than to offer different prices in parallel to different buyers.

EXPANDING INTO AN ENTERPRISE-WIDE DEAL

Happy customers buy more. With a functional, expandable pricing model and an active customer success function that helps the customer adopt and expand their usage, you'll get the customer to be the one who initiates the customization conversation. For example, if you have a $500,000 contract with HR, a $300,000 deal with Operations, and an $800,000 contract with Marketing (each paid for out of their department budget), it's likely that someone in the other company's Finance or IT department will see these sizeable costs. Inevitably, they'll want to negotiate a combined purchase. In that case, you as the vendor will have a better negotiating position: each of the departments is already using, paying for, and getting value from your product. The customer could threaten to walk away. Still, the cost of switching from your solution to a competitor's—and the dissatisfaction of the people who already love your product—means that you can negotiate from a stronger position. Start small, make them happy, and they'll come back for more.

When that happens, structure a multiyear deal. Most contracts are yearly, but if you can, push for a three-year contract with a renegotiation afterwards. But for that sneaky customer who wants a most-favored-nations (MFN) deal for three years with a term of convenience after 12 months to cancel, then politely say no. Any company wanting an MFN wants you to do a lot of their work with little return. In nearly all instances, you should decline to enter an MFN deal. But certainly, try to get that multiyear deal, especially when they are satisfied with your product.

Once you execute that contract, start making the martinis. Execute your handoffs and the trifecta of project, relationship, and pricing management. Your lighthouse will serve as your marquee account, not only signaling to others in the market that you are the leader, but also letting others know how wonderful your service is. If that happens, your sales and BD team may not even have to knock on another door. You've landed the ship and expanded around the lighthouse; now finding new accounts on the way to transformational deals will be a breeze.

All of that in Part 3 was the secret sauce.

GO FOR IT AND CONNECT THE WORLD

CONGRATULATIONS! YOU COMPLETED THE JOURNEY!

Thank you for reading my book. I'm honored you finished it. Let's review and get on with building companies.

When you are staring across the chasm, looking at lighthouse deals and doubting you can reach them, follow my approach to allay your fears and chart your course. Do it and don't look back. Like I did at the beginning of this book, just go for it.

Here's how.

Part 1: Chart Your Course

Know the signs that you are approaching the chasm and consider how to reorganize your GTM team to navigate it. Don't fret! Step back and get a bird's-eye view of the lay of the land. Analyze your potential targets and the competition. Contemplate your strategy vis-à-vis the competitors and how to use BD as a tool to outsmart them. With that information, put together your story and a few pitch decks. Now, you are ready to test the waters, gain market feedback, and alter your strategy and plans. Recall what Eisenhower said: "Plans are useless, but planning is indispensable.

Part 2: Galvanize Your Crew and Maneuver Strategically

With your lighthouses more clearly visible in the distance, make deal plans for how you will reach them. What's measured is managed, and this is the way to manage your progress. Both international positioning and corporate development are ways to maneuver your ship into an advantage. Once in position, excite your crew and get them ready! Herein, they will be part of your execution team. They will help you with international execution, PR and marketing, and pricing tactics. An all-hands-on-deck approach at this stage readies the team for what's to come and allows easy sailing in to the dock.

Part 3: Land and Expand

Now it's time to land the ship at the lighthouse. The best captains navigate through choppy seas, darkness, and fog with a level-headed commitment to get the deal done. Throw emotions overboard and focus on the five Cs of closing. First, be a *consultant*, showing them they both need you and like you. Create a collegial atmosphere of *collaboration* and mutual respect. Get them to *commit* to you through some type of verbal agreement. Then, *close* it out by using negotiation tactics of empathy and respect. Don't count your money until the *customer success* team sings!

Follow this approach, and you will succeed with little chance of error. That's why I wrote the book! Land that deal and catapult your company across the chasm into a new market with bigger players, bigger opportunities, and bigger revenues on the way to an initial public offering (IPO). I hope the book helps you do all this, or at the very least, that it serves as a compendium of useful information about BD that was worth your time and the few shekels that you spent. But BD is not all about the money, is it?

Do Deals to Connect the World

Last, I'd like to impart some personal wisdom in all this money-making rah-rah. Find meaning in your work. It's different for every person, but strategic BD was worth it for me because it was intellectually rewarding; it afforded me the opportunity to see the world; and it allowed me to make that world a better place.

Figuring out how to get a product to market after many failed attempts is mentally stimulating. Rarely does a BD strategy work perfectly at the outset. A BD Captain must find several ways to get to the right contact, offer different product solutions, and learn how to steer conversations to their advantage. Learning how to pick yourself up, dust yourself off, and try again with a different approach is a skill for a lifetime. Thinking through the myriad of options and strategies will keep your mind churning into the wee hours of the night.

Business development showed me the world. My job afforded me the chance to go places, experience new cultures, and meet interesting people I never dreamed I'd meet. I spent ample time working across Asia, throughout different countries in Europe, and in the Middle East. I was blessed to get this opportunity, especially before the pandemic.

Business development builds bridges across the globe. The deals I made allowed companies separated by vast seas to work closely together to reach a shared mission. To achieve these successful partnerships, companies with very different cultures and business practices, regulated by different laws, had to work hand in hand. It was a giant undertaking that connected consumers, companies, and countries. That's meaningful.

The more global deals we do, the more the world will assimilate and get along. Friction is inevitable, but cultural differences fall by the wayside when working toward a shared goal. Building a company bridges people. Business deals bridge companies. Together they drive government policy, and those policies connect countries. The more cross-company and cross-border relationships we facilitate, the more likely we are to remain at peace. I wholeheartedly believe this.

So get on with it! Now, it is your turn to be an ambassador: go out and connect the world with technology and business partnerships. The seas you navigate will be choppy and turbulent at times, but don't give up. Find a guiding light to direct you through the vast ocean. Build an amazing team to go on that journey. Be persistent, yet polite, in your business deals, and those lighthouse deals may find you before you find them. Good luck!

ENDNOTES

1   Geoffrey A. Moore, *Crossing the Chasm* (New York: Harper Business, 2014), 11.

2   Moore, *Crossing the Chasm*, 21.

3   Peter Thiel and Blake Masters, *Zero to One: Notes on Startups, or How to Build the Future* (New York: Crown Business, 2014), 128.

4   Clayton Christensen, *The Innovator's Dilemma* (Boston: Harvard Business Review, 2016), 25.

5   Ben Horowitz, *The Hard Thing about Hard Things* (New York: Harper Business, 2014), 171.

6   James Clear, "First Principles: Elon Musk on the Power of Thinking for Yourself," https://jamesclear.com/first-principles, August 1, 2021.

7   *Ten Years of Burrowing in the Netherlands East Indies* (New York: Netherlands Information Bureau, 1942), 49. As seen on the Papua website, http://papuaweb.org/dlib/nei/nei-1942-japanese-burrowing-nei.pdf, accessed August 1, 2021.

8   Robert Cialdini, *Influence: The Psychology of Persuasion* (New York: Harper Business, 2006), e-book location 1007.

9   As seen on the Quote to Spark website, https://quotestospark.com/famous-confucius-quotes/, accessed August 1, 2021.

10   https://www.oxfordreference.com/view/10.1093/acref/9780191826719.001.0001/q-oro-ed4-00004005

11   Bill Reiter, "How Stephen Curry Ushered in the NBA's Greatest Shooting Era and Changed Perception of Championship Teams," CBS Sports website, June 20, 2020.

12   Orlando Silva, "Kirk Goldsberry Explains How the Game Has Changed from 2001 to 2020," Fadeaway World, January 15, 2020, https://fadeawayworld.net/nba-media/kirk-goldsberry-explains-how -the-game-has-changed-from-2001-to-2020.

13   Erika Anderson, "21 Quotes from Henry Ford on Business, Leadership, and Life," *Forbes*, last modified May 13, 2013, https://www.forbes.com/ sites/erikaandersen/2013/05/31/21-quotes-from-henry-ford-on-business- leadership-and-life/?sh=3fc45ee1293c.

14   Jerry Chen, "Unit of Value: A Framework for Scaling," Greylock, January 26, 2016, https://news.greylock.com/unit-of-value-a-framework -for-scaling-42c092fba887.

15   Bob Burg, The Art of Persuasion (Shippensburg: Sound Wisdom, 2011), 138.

16   Cialdini, *Influence*, e-book location 348.

17   As seen on the Smule website, https://www.smule.com/song/tom-cruise -cuba-gooding-jr-jerry-maguire-help-me-help-you-karaoke-lyrics/ 488448690_508732/arrangement, accessed August 1, 2021.

18   Chris Voss and Tahl Raz, *Never Split the Difference* (New York: Harper Business, 2016), 54.

19   Kathleen M. Eisenhardt, Jean L. Kahwajy, and L. J. Bourgeois III, "How Management Teams Can Have a Good Fight," *Harvard Business Review*, July–August 1997, 80.

CPSIA information can be obtained
at www.ICGtesting.com
Printed in the USA
JSHW051358180922
30577JS00001B/7